Remembering
The Indian School

**Recollections of life at the
Winnebago Indian Mission School
Neillsville, Wisconsin**

1926-2003

**Jacob C. Stucki
2004**

Copyright © 2004 by Jacob C. Stucki

ISBN 0-7414-1894-0

Published by:

PUBLISHING.COM

519 West Lancaster Avenue
Haverford, PA 19041-1413
Info@buybooksontheweb.com
www.buybooksontheweb.com
Toll-free (877) BUY BOOK
Local Phone (610) 520-2500
Fax (610) 519-0261

Printed in the United States of America

Printed on Recycled Paper

Published January 2004

Table of Contents

Chapter I – First Remembrances

On November 30, 1926, an Alberta Clipper roared across the Midwest creating huge, deadly waves on Lake Superior and a roaring snowstorm in Wisconsin. The Great Lakes shipping season was ending as it always does in late November or early December, with a few commercial vessels making a last chancy trip before ice clogs the ports and the waterways. Some of the vessels made it to profitable destinations. Others did not.

One of the unlucky ones was the City of Bangor bound from Detroit to Duluth with a cargo of new 1926 Chryslers. She ran aground on a pile of rocks in Lake Superior between Keweenaw Point and Copper Harbor and split open. The engine room was flooded. There she sat gradually freezing in place in the subzero temperature. Eighteen of the Chryslers located on the deck were blown into the lake by the fierce wind. After the lake had frozen solid enough, the remaining cars were driven off the ship and over the ice to Copper Harbor for eventual return to Detroit where they were repaired and resold. Although the crew of the City of Bangor survived, they suffered greatly from frostbite and exhaustion.

November 30, 1926, is also the date when I was born. I was born at our home on the Winnebago Indian School Campus. I don't remember anything of that experience, of course, but I do have other early memories of life at the School.

My earliest memories were fixed by trivial events, significant only to me. The Old Mission at Black River Falls, Wisconsin, is about 25 miles from the Indian School at Neillsville, Wisconsin. A close relationship between administrators of the two Missions required a great deal of travel between Neillsville and Black River Falls. My parents made their trips in an open-sided Model T Ford.

Sister Marie and I were riding home from the Old Mission to Neillsville with our parents. Mom was in the front seat with Dad who was driving. Marie and I were in the back seat. The side curtains were open because the weather was beautiful. As we were driving along the dusty, two-rutted road running through the Mission, I tumbled out of the car onto a pile of brush. I remember the occasion vividly. I was less than 2 years old (sister Peg had not yet been born). I remember sitting on the pile of brush watching the Model T disappearing down the road. I remember being astonished but not afraid.

Meanwhile, Marie (so I am told) began fussing in the back seat. She was crying and saying, "Kebbie's gone, Kebbie's gone!" Kebbie is a somewhat garbled, German diminutive of the name Jacob. Marie was 20 months my senior. Finally Mom turned around and saw that Kebbie indeed was gone! "He fell out," sobbed Marie. Dad stopped the car, turned around and rushed back. When he got to me I was still sitting on the brush pile none the worse for wear.

The second memory was imprinted by a seemingly unimportant but mind-boggling disclosure. The Indian School had a sidewalk running all the way around the main building. This sidewalk was perfect for roller-skating and the like. One day some Indian boys were pulling me around the building in a coaster wagon. As we reached the door to the 'boys' side' of the building, one of the young Indian lads said to me, "Did you know that you father puts his 'thing' into your mother's 'thing'?" I replied, "Why would he do that?" The boy answered, "How do you think you got here?" Then he explained to me the mechanics of human sexual reproduction in graphic detail. I was astounded to say the least, but also deeply interested and excited. I was about 3 years old. Thus began my life-long fascination with human sexuality both in theory and in practice. I married Naomi Bersch in 1948. We remain married to this date. We have three children and two grandchildren. In 1954 I was awarded

2

a Ph.D. degree in Zoology from the University of Wisconsin. My thesis was entitled, *The Relationship of Adrenal Cortical Hormones and Pregnancy in the Rat as Evaluated by Consideration of Inflammatory Phenomenon.*

I have a vivid memory of the wagon and its exact position on the sidewalk when the bombshell dropped. Several years later Dad gave me a lecture on the birds and the bees. I listened respectfully and had no questions when he asked me if I understood everything. The lecture really was about the birds and the bees, or at least the bees, for what he told me was about flower pollination and the role of the bees in this process. He never told me anything else about reproduction, but the school had a farm. It is difficult to remain ignorant on a farm.

Another early memory was imprinted when I drove (steered) my maternal grandfather's Model T off a stone retaining wall. The Model T had been parked in our driveway headed downhill. I climbed into the front seat, managed to release the parking brake and as the car slowly gained speed in the dozen or so yards to a curve with a drop-off to a terrace beneath a stone wall, I tried to steer the car around the corner to no avail. Off the wall we went. Only the fact that the underside of the chassis hung up on the wall saved me from disaster. It did not save me from Grandpa Kuester's wrath. This was my first driving experience. I was perhaps 4 years old. By the time I was ten, I had learned how to drive our Model T on the school and farm roads. I could barely reach the pedals.

What follows is an account of life at the Indian School as experienced by me. This is not a heavily researched account. It is drawn mostly from my memory and as such probably includes distortions and certainly errors of omission and commission. I hope my relatives and childhood friends will forgive these errors. I look forward to reading their versions of this interesting period in our lives.

Chapter II – The Indian School

Life with the Indians at the Neillsville Indian School and the Old Mission at Black River Falls cannot be fully appreciated without a more detailed account of how Grandfather Stucki (Grosspapa) and Dad came to serve these two institutions. Grosspapa was born on January 23, 1857, in Diemtigen, Canton Berne, Switzerland, to a single mother who deserted him. He lived a life of poverty in the Bernese highlands in the care of his maternal grandmother. He was 13 when his grandmother died and left him alone. His grandmother had not neglected his formal and religious education. He had been baptized, attended primary and secondary school and, in 1872, was confirmed into the fellowship of the Reformed Church. Essentially alone in the world, he was helped by the village schoolmaster to immigrate to America and to get a job with a Toledo, Ohio, nurseryman and his wife. He arrived in Toledo on May 22, 1873.

He worked diligently at the greenhouse and nursery and paid back, out of his earnings, all of the money advanced him. He was said by his employer to be the best worker he had ever seen. He continued his secular education in Toledo public schools and his religious education in the First Reformed Church in Toledo, under the pastoral leadership of Rev. Christopher Schiller who urged him to study for the ministry. In 1877, Grosspapa entered the Mission House in Plymouth, Wisconsin, as a divinity student. In 1884 he accepted an assignment as assistant to Jacob Hauser, chief missionary, at the Indian Mission near Black River Falls, Wisconsin. The Sheboygan Classis of the Reformed Church had founded the Mission in 1878.

My Dad, Benjamin Stucki, or Mr. Ben as he was called, was Grosspapa's third son, born in 1893. After an education at the Mission House Academy and College, and a stint at the University of California at Berkeley, Dad and his older

4

brother Cal, also at Berkeley, patriotically joined the Army to fight the Hun. Dad and Cal both served in the medical corps.

Immediately after the war, Uncle Cal completed his medical education and became a medical missionary in China, but Dad was asked to interrupt his education to build and establish a boarding school at Neillsville for the Indians. Dad was architect, principal contractor and construction superintendent all in one, all skills he learned on the job. At one time I had a ledger that recorded project expenditures right down to the nails and the horse team rentals. It was a study in detail and exemplified the care with which Dad always handled other people's money. I gave this ledger to the Wisconsin State Historical Society some years ago. Building and opening the school was to have been a temporary job, but when construction was completed, Dad was asked to become superintendent. He never succeeded in leaving and died at the Indian School, still working, in 1961.

The lives of both Grosspapa and Dad are described in a variety of publications such as *The Swiss in the United States* by John Paul von Grueningen, 1940, Swiss-American Historical Society, and *The Winnebago Finds a Friend* by Arthur V. Casselman, 1946, Board of National Missions Evangelical and Reformed Church. In 2003, my daughter Marcia and I compiled and edited a collection of letters written by a schoolteacher at the Old Mission. *Miss Emma Manthe's Letters* provides another version of life at the Old Mission at the turn of the century (1900).

Perhaps the most important thing about Dad and Grosspapa was the origin of their religious beliefs. They came from a Calvinist tradition, Grosspapa more than Dad. Calvin's catechism requires people to place emphasis on both their relationship with God and their relationship with other people. Calvinists are admonished to pay equal attention to the commandments of the Lord regarding worship and to charitable acts towards their neighbors. It was probably this latter admonition that caused Grosspapa and Dad to have such overwhelming interest in helping the Indians, not only to know "the true faith", but also to have a satisfying and abundant life. They preached the social and economic gospel as well as the gospel of Christian faith.

The Indian Schools at the Old Mission and in Neillsville were only two of many schools for Indians established and operated in the years 1850-1950. Many of the schools were built and operated by the Federal government whose policy makers had concluded that it was cheaper to educate Indians than to eradicate them. In most government schools and, sad to say, in some church-based schools as well, the education consisted of equal parts of indoctrination into the ways of the white man and the abolition of the tribal culture. In such schools the children were discouraged from speaking their native languages and were constantly reminded that their ways were inferior to those of the whites. The goal of their education was preparation for assimilation into white society, but not complete assimilation, for even an educated Indian was considered inferior. The hope was that educated Indians would work and thus eliminate their need for government support. To some extent this strategy worked but the plight of Native Americans remains comparatively dismal.

English was the language of instruction at the Neillsville Indian School, but conversation in the Winnebago language was neither prohibited nor discouraged. Grosspapa, Dad and all his siblings spoke excellent Winnebago. With the help of John Stacy, Grosspapa translated several books of the Bible into Winnebago

The Indian Mission School was located on a fertile farm in the western part of the city of Neillsville on the Black River. Neillsville is situated on the transition zone between a fertile glacier deposit on the north and a dry prehistoric lake bottom on the south. The lake had long disappeared leaving only sand and plants that could survive low soil fertility and moisture. The flora of this prehistoric lake region was interesting and provided more than one botany graduate student with material for a thesis. My cousin, Frank Grether, was one such student.

The Old Mission is near the town of Black River Falls, about 25 miles southwest of Neillsville, in the heart of sand country. The Mission was located there because that was where the United States Government dumped the Winnebago Indians. After being driven from their fertile lands in southern Wisconsin and northern Illinois they were moved from reservation to reservation, then moved again as each new reservation became coveted by the white man.

The Historical Marker on I-94 south of Black River Falls, erected in 1974, tells some of their story. It reads as follows:

"WINNEBAGO INDIANS"

"Winnebago Indians call themselves "Hochunkgra." A Siouan people, they once occupied the southern half of Wisconsin and the northern counties of Illinois. The Black Hawk War of 1832 and a series of treaties forced the Winnebago out of their homeland, and they were removed to reservations in Iowa, Minnesota, South Dakota, and finally to a portion of the Omaha Reservation in Nebraska.

With each removal, small bands of Winnebago returned to Wisconsin, with the largest settlement in Jackson County. About seven miles east of Black River Falls is the historic Winnebago Indian Mission, founded by the German Reformed Church in 1878. The Mission included about half of the Winnebago population of Jackson County, the pow-wow grounds, Indian Cemetery and Mitchell Red Cloud Memorial.

Tribal traditions are preserved through the clan system, the Medicine Lodge, and War Bundle Feast."

The rest of the story is still being played out. In 1875, after considerable public indignation, the U. S. Government allowed the Jackson County band of Winnebago Indians to take up land in approximately forty-acre units. The land was virtually useless for agriculture. According to my Dad, the Indian land was encumbered by sales and inheritance restrictions but was to be tax-free for a period of years. At the end of the tax-free period, notices of taxes due were published together with notices that any tax-delinquent property would be taken into the State Forest with no rights of repossession by the owners upon payment of the delinquent taxes. Most of the Indians (and many others) lost (or sold) their property to the State of Wisconsin.

The Indian Mission is located in Section 33 of Komensky Township. Most of the Indian property was located in sections 14, 22, 28, 29, 32 and 34. Examination of some old plat maps of Jackson County showed the ownership of land in sections 13-17 and 20-36 of Komensky Township, to be virtually all privately owned in 1919. Using obvious Indian names as a guide, I estimate that Indians held title to at least 1,680 acres of the 14,080 acres in these sections in 1919. By 1972, Indians owned about 360 acres in those sections, and by 2003, 640 acres. Plat maps are often inaccurate so these figures should be used with caution.

Something appears to have happened that permitted the return of some State Forest land to Indian ownership. The recognition of the Wisconsin Winnebago Tribe by the Federal Government and changing attitudes towards Indians may have accounted in part for this change, but I suspect that the increased financial and political power of the tribe following their entry into the casino business may have been more important than recognition and changing attitudes.

The Neillsville Indian School campus and farms were situated on both banks of the Black River and on both sides of U. S. Highway 10 (now County Trunk B). Highway 10 ran east and west, roughly perpendicular to the river. At the site of the school, the river valley was about a mile and a half from top to top. The vistas were gorgeous. Highway 10 ran up the hill from the river bottom for about a mile to the western top of the valley. Highway 10 went under a railroad overpass located about a third of the way to the top. The railroad roughly paralleled the river and marked the western boundary of the school's farm property. About a quarter of a mile northeast of the overpass, the railroad crossed the river on a high steel trestle. From the river, Highway 10 ran east to the top of the hill about a quarter-mile from the school.

The boundary of the school farm property on the east was the top of the river valley. The southern boundary crossed the river south of the highway bridge in an area where the river was wide and shallow. The eastern bank of the river at the junction of the river and the highway was a steep and rocky cliff. The cliff, when seen from the riverbank, looked like the stone face of an Indian Chief wearing a large headdress. This seemed a fitting image for an Indian School. The northern boundary was originally Highway 10, but land on the north side of the highway was purchased sometime in the 1940s, making the river the northern boundary. Some of this property was used to build a new house for my parents in the early 1950s. I estimate the entire school property to have been about 160 acres.

In my youth, the property was a young adventurer's dream. It included a river, two farms, wood lots, scrap heaps, junk piles, barns and other farm outbuildings, a well, a milk house, horses and cows, hogs, cats and dogs, chickens, a climbing cliff and two bridges – one for the highway and one for the railroad. There were fields of hay and other crops, two gigantic truck gardens to feed the staff and students – and our family. Part of Dad's salary was paid in the form of groceries. This meant that our family never had to worry about having enough to eat, not even in the 'Depression.' There were fish and other animals in the river in abundance. There were also other things in the river. Upstream from the school, the city of Neillsville dumped raw sewerage into the river. Some surprising things would float down the river when it was low in the summer.

The house in which we lived was on school property on Highway 10 partway up the hill toward downtown. It was a big white farmhouse overlooking the river valley, the two bridges and the main school building.

Hills were a prominent feature of the entire property. The main building was located on a hill, the top of which had been made flat by moving large amounts of dirt. This was accomplished using horses and slide buckets maneuvered into taking bites from the earth by a combination of manual effort and horsepower. Immediately south of the building, toward the river, the flat land dropped steeply, providing a wonderful venue for sliding and for kick-the-can. Halfway down the hill were the septic tanks. The effluent from the tanks emptied into the river. The place where the tanks emptied was the most productive fishing spot in the whole river. On the crest of the hill near the kitchen entrance was a large concrete, steel and brick incinerator for burning trash.

Another old farmhouse was located right next to the main building. It was used for storage and 'Manual Training' (carpentry mostly) for the boys. The girls learned sewing and other domestic arts in a large room on the third floor of the main building. The basement of the Manual Training building contained bins for storing potatoes, turnips, carrots and barrels of pickles and sauerkraut.

The wood lots south of the main building located along the river were called, "the first woods," "the second woods," and "the third woods." The Indian School owned only "the first woods." All "woods" bordered on the river and were extensions of the property owned by others. A common tree in the "first woods" was the butternut.

Each wood lot was bordered by a fence that paralleled the river and by fences that ran perpendicular to the river. The first woods were ours but when we ventured into the other woods, we were in alien territory.

The first perpendicular fence along the first woods divided the northern edge of the woods from a field directly south of the Indian School main building. A red shale-covered road went around the entire building in those days, and on the backside of the building, the side toward the river and the woods, the shoulder of the road dropped off steeply toward the field and the river.

In the summertime when I was about ten, I would fish in the Black River with a cane pole. Sometimes I would put a large streamer fly on the end of the line and then wade the river with my rig. I would fling the streamer out by rocks and sand bars and jerk it along by moving the pole. Often I was rewarded with a large mouth bass or a walleye or maybe a rock bass. My Dad and his brothers, Uncle Heinie and Uncle Jack, would fish the river with fly rods that allowed them to make the fly move by pulling the line rather than the pole. Sometimes they would catch muskies or northern pike.

The best fishing for me would be on hot July afternoons when I would take my pole and a jar with holes in the cover and head for the river through the fields. On my way I caught a supply of large grasshoppers for bait. With my freshly caught bait I'd go to the place in the river where the septic tank emptied. There the fish were always big and fat.

I would take these fish home and we would eat them with impunity. In the summer when I fished, there were only a few people at the school so the septic system was not overloaded. I imagine the fish were really quite healthy and only swam in the septic effluent because of the temperature differential to the river water.

The river was wide, shallow and rocky. At times we could cross the river on the rocks without getting out feet wet simply by "jumping rocks" as we called it. At other times the river was a raging flood that could carry away anything.

The first woods were used as a pasture by the cows and horses so the grass in it was always closely cropped and there was little underbrush. The trees were large with high branches and were rather more far apart than is usual in mature forests. I think some of the trees must have been harvested for firewood to keep the woods sparse enough to serve as pasture. When dead limbs would drop, they would be picked up and put on a large pile by the barn to be sawed into short lengths by hand or with a circular saw powered in the early years by a small, one-cylinder, gas engine and later by the tractor.

Dad enjoyed hunting squirrels in the first woods. Sometimes I would hunt with him - without a gun. The squirrels were very cagey and would move slowly around the tree trunk when being hunted so the hunter couldn't locate them. With two people, sometimes you could fool the squirrel. More often than not, however, the squirrel would remain on the side of the tree facing the person who didn't have the gun. Me. My Dad used a Savage, bolt action, .22 rim-fire rifle for hunting squirrels. It was a beautiful gun and he was very proud of it. Many people hunted squirrel with a shotgun. Dad never did. He would always "aim for the head" when hunting squirrels and that way not spoil the meat. He had nothing but contempt for anyone who hunted squirrel with a shotgun.

Dad didn't even own a shotgun and so he couldn't hunt game birds in the way everyone else did. Sometimes he would get a roosting partridge, through the head, of course, while he was squirrel hunting.

We really liked to play in the first woods. It was cool there and we always felt "safe." This was in stark contrast to how we felt in the second and third woods. They belonged to someone else and we never knew when someone might surprise us while we were engaging in some important project.

One time we decided to build a tree house along the river in the second woods. We had a hatchet, a hammer and some nails and fashioned the tree house from small saplings we chopped down and nailed across large branches in the tree. In this way we made a primitive sort of floor in the tree. We were sitting in the tree cutting a sapling to length for the floor when "The Enemy" appeared in the form of the middle-aged son of the owner of the woods. He had a ferocious demeanor, or so we thought. I hesitated in mid swing and we eyed each other - I fearful, he menacing. Finally he grinned and said, "Well, hurry up and chop!" I did.

One September afternoon some of the Indian boys and I were playing in the first woods. At the back end of the woods by the river was a dump of sorts. Various things like old fencing and useless lumber were dumped there to rot or get carried away by the high water. In this dump we found an old five-gallon can that seemed to be in pretty good shape.

We pondered at length what to do with the can and finally decided we would build a fire and make a stew just like the hobos did in the movies we saw on Saturday afternoon at the theatre in town.

No sooner said than done. Somebody had matches to light the fire. We gathered stones for a fire ring and in no time we had a pot of river water boiling. What to put in the stew? Three blocks away was the school building and immediately east of the building along the road between the barn and the building was the garden that Uncle Jack cultivated for the Indian School. We ambled up to the garden and sneakily picked some carrots, kohlrabi, tomatoes and other ripe vegetables. On the way back to the fire we stopped in the cornfield and picked some Evergreen white sweet corn. Everything was then hacked up and dumped into the stew pot.

But we were missing meat. What to do? Finally we went down to the river and caught a bunch of crayfish, the kind that are green and swim backwards. They are easy enough to catch if you lift up a few rocks. We also picked some river clams from the river bottom. Into the pot the clams and crayfish went. And then a most amazing thing happened! The crayfish turned red!

I had never seen a shrimp or a lobster, of course, and nobody ever ate crayfish, so I had no occasion to see one cooked. Therefore, I had no idea that green shellfish turned red when boiled. I can remember being quite astonished.

The stew smelled wonderful as it cooked, but for a variety of reasons, none of us wanted to partake. For one thing, we hadn't been particularly careful in cleaning the vegetables, and they had gone in sand, roots, tops and all. And then there were those clams and crayfish. They smelled real good but we didn't know if they were fit to eat or not. Could have been poison or something, you know.

So we upended the can and spilled all the stew on the ground, clams, red crayfish and all. But we still had a fire and were beginning to get hungry, so we went to the nearby field and picked some ripe "field" corn.

It is important to know that while field corn is ripe and hard in September, Evergreen sweet corn is still soft. I think the Evergreen is planted a lot later than ordinary corn. It was a favorite at the Indian School because it could be served to the kids when they returned to school in September. By that time the Golden Bantam and other sweet corns were long past.

Anyway, field corn is the raw material for "cook-corn," a kind of ersatz popcorn that is made in a tin tomato can with holes punched in the bottom. Cook-corn is pretty tough and hard to eat, but it does smell good and tastes terrific. Try to imagine eating only the Old-Maids when you make popcorn. That's "cook-corn." Anyway, we went back to the dump, picked up a useable tomato can, punched holes in the bottom with a rusty nail, attached a split stick to serve as a handle, dumped in some field corn kernels, and cooked our supper over the open fire. It was super! We felt just like tramps.

****

Other hills on school property began on the eastern crest of the river valley and ended at the riverbank. The distance from the crest to the river was a quarter to a half-mile. This was an outstanding sledding and skiing hill. We made our own sleds in Manual Training and instead of skis we used barrel staves. These were used as singles rather than pairs and were really primitive snowboards.

Halfway up this hill and set into the hill a most interesting building. The lowest part of the building was a hog house. Next to the hog house in the same building was a slaughterhouse. The second story of this building was a machine shed reached by a ramp with stone walls much like the stone wall that trapped my grandfather's Model T, only much higher. These walls were about eight feet high. The machine shed contained a host of interesting things, not the least of which was the dynamite cache. Dynamite was used to blast stumps out of the ground. In the absence of power equipment, dynamite was sometimes the only alternative with a truly large and stubborn stump that couldn't be removed by horsepower. The farmer showed me where the dynamite was hidden when I was about 10. He didn't tell me where the fuses and blasting caps were located.

South of the hog house was the hog pen where the hogs could sun themselves, root around in the dirt and eat the garbage that was routinely dumped over the fence. That garbage included kitchen scraps and the offal from butchering in the slaughterhouse. Organized cannibalism for the sake of fattening the livestock did not first begin in the second half of the 20th century as epidemiologists might have us believe as they try to account for the emergence of mad cow disease and its human counterpart. It is important to note that hogs are omnivorous and offal is a natural food for them, while cattle are herbivores and have to be taught to eat their fellow beings. Not that pigs eating pigs is necessarily benign. This practice also leads to diseases spread from hog to hog that are passed on to man. So I think the practice of feeding offal to hogs is also prohibited most places.

Down the hill from the machine shed was the barn and the silo. A hayloft topped the barn and a granary room was in the barn next to the silo chute through which the silage was retrieved and fed to the cows. At the west end of the barn was a door through which the cows came for milking. The horses were also located in this barn as were the calves.

This barn was quite modern with a high rounded roof covering the hayloft. No beams interrupted the hayloft space so that hay and straw could be piled wherever desired. Also, the floor of the hayloft was solid wood, probably two-layered with tarpaper in between the layers of wood. I believe the barn was built in the early 1920s. Sometime in the late 30's the barn caught fire. Only the hayloft and the roof were destroyed. The ground floor survived, as did all of the animals housed in the barn. Apparently water sprayed into the hayloft collected on the hayloft floor and prevented the fire from spreading to the ground floor. I'll never forget the night the barn burned. I was there watching all the action.

****

The Neillsville firemen were all volunteers and they were having their monthly beer and card party when the alarm came. That was the good news. They were all assembled in one place and all got the same message -- where to go and how to get there; what was burning and what kind of equipment to bring. Ordinarily, the firemen came from all over the town. Some came from their homes where they were sleeping or eating. Some came from their businesses or places of work. Some were not even in town and so they couldn't respond at all to the fire call. This was how volunteer firemen worked. They did it for love of the community and for adventure, not for pay.

The bad news was that by the time the alarm came, the firemen had consumed more beer than they could possibly metabolize. Beer-drenched firemen don't always make the best decisions. Sometimes they get messages mixed up and sometimes they simply don't get the message, or if they do, they respond inappropriately. That's what happened the night the barn burned.

Someone had seen the fire shortly after it started and had immediately released the animals inside the barn and phoned the fire department. The barn was not very far from the firehouse, but the fire hydrant was one block closer to the center of town than was the burning barn.

The fire truck is usually parked between the hydrant and the fire. The firemen use one hose to connect the truck to the hydrant and another hose to carry water from the truck to the fire. The hydrant is opened and the water starts running into the pump in the fire truck. The pump in the fire truck starts up and puts a huge amount of pressure on the water coming from the hydrant so that the water can shoot out of the nozzle at the fire end of the hose with a great deal of force.

Well, this time the fire truck driver drove the fire truck right up to the barn. Then all the firemen got out of the truck and admired the fire. They hadn't seen such a nice fire for a long time. Suddenly one of the firemen remembered that they were supposed to put out the fire and he yelled, "Water! We need water!" The other firemen leapt into the truck and sped back to the hydrant.

The driver parked the truck right next to the hydrant and the firemen jumped out and hooked up the hose to the hydrant. Then they hooked a hose up to the other side of the pump in the truck, turned on the water and the pump and pulled the hose toward the barn. Darn! The hose was too short to reach the fire!

The firemen ran back to the truck and the driver got in and drove toward the barn, but he didn't calculate properly the length of the hose between the truck and the hydrant. All of a sudden he was farther away from the hydrant than the hose would allow and with a loud pop and a roar of water the hose snapped! The driver swore, stopped the pump and drove the truck back to the hydrant. The firemen quickly shut off the water, removed the broken hose and placed a new hose between the hydrant and the truck. Then the driver very carefully drove the truck toward the barn. All of the other firemen were watching the hose between the hydrant and the truck very carefully and when the truck was the proper distance from the hydrant so that the hose would be as long as possible but wouldn't break, they shouted at the driver to stop. The driver was sweating bullets by that time because there were no more extra hoses on the truck and if he broke this one, it was all over!

This time the driver stopped in time, but soon discovered that while he was driving back and forth, the other hose, the one between the truck and the fire, was being dragged back and forth and had been run over several times by the moving truck. In fact, it was fairly badly tangled up under the truck by that time.

The firemen cursed some more and crawled under the truck to disentangle the hose. Finally the hose was free and stretched out to the fire. Everything was now set to fight the fire. One end of a hose was attached to the hydrant and the other end was attached to the pump on the fire truck. The fire truck was as close to the fire as it could get without breaking the hose. The other hose, the one with the fire-fighting nozzle, was attached to the other side of the pump on the truck and the nozzle end of the hose was by the burning barn.

The firemen were now all at the fire. Some of them were holding the hose and some of them were just standing around doing nothing at this point. They were ready to fight the fire, but no water was coming out of the hose.

"Water! Water!" cried the firemen holding the hose.

Suddenly one of the firemen who had not had so much beer to drink as the others realized that the hydrant had not been turned on again. So he shouted, "The hydrant! The hydrant!" The firemen came to life and ran back to the hydrant. After a while they found the wrench that was used to open and close the valve. Somebody had dropped it in the weeds after closing the valve when the first hose broke. They opened the valve again and the water surged toward the truck. The firemen ran back to the fire, but still no water came out of the nozzle.

"Water! Water!" cried the firemen.

By this time the firemen had run back and forth so much that the beer they had consumed was pretty much metabolized away, so they were all more alert and all realized more or less at the same time that they had forgotten to start the pump in the fire truck. So they ran back to the truck and started the pump.

The water finally came shooting out of the nozzle, and they pointed it at the fire.

I hope my readers and the good people of Neillsville will forgive the obvious exaggeration and fictionalization of events at the fire. The scene was just too funny to relate objectively and truthfully. Not all of the firemen ran to all of the events as I portrayed them, but the cries of "Water, water" were real as I remember, as were some of the mistakes in setting up the equipment. This was not surprising given the fact that the firemen were volunteers and didn't get all that much practice. Actually, the firemen performed very competently that night and succeeded in confining the fire to the hayloft and saving the ground floor of the barn. The damaged part of the barn was rebuilt to its original form.

****

Immediately north of the barn was the henhouse with roosts made of saplings and wooden nest boxes. A large feed box was located in the one-room building. Openings near the floor permitted the hens to go out into the fenced-in yard where they could scratch and seek out bugs and worms, things that made the eggs taste good.

West of the barn was a small milk house cooled by a nearby spring. The milk house was about 150 yards down the hill from our house. The fresh milk was stored in the milk house in 20-gallon milk cans set in concrete compartments through which fresh spring water constantly ran. The spring that fed the milk house was located halfway between our house and the milk house. It was simply a hole dug into a natural spring coming out of a hill immediately to the north of the hen house. A concrete igloo-like structure with a locked entrance door covered the entire spring. Water flowed from the spring pit directly to the milk house via an underground pipe.

The 'igloo' door opened to an eight-foot deep cavity with a steel ladder reaching to the bottom of the pit. Several times a year the door was unlocked and the farmer went down into the pit with buckets and other cleaning gear. He made certain that all dead frogs and other contaminants were removed together with all residual water. Then he scoured the rocks lining the bottom of the pit and finally allowed the spring to once again flow.

The farmhouse and outbuildings on the property on the west side of the river were from an earlier time. The house lacked running water and electricity when I first became aware of it, but these amenities were added later. The barn was a two-story post and beam type of building probably constructed at the turn of the century. All of the skeletal elements of the building were held together with wooden pegs. The vertical barn boards were nailed to the beams. The barn floor was dirt. In addition to the house and the barn there were some dilapidated machine sheds and corncribs. The school purchased this farm sometime in the 30's. A small stream wandered through the pasture west of the farmhouse. It originated someplace on the other side of the railroad tracks and flowed through a culvert under the tracks. A truck garden was located in the fertile, flat ground between the house and the river on the east.

****

The main building on the campus, built in two phases in 1920 and 1924, was a 3-story, 23,000-square-foot brick building with a tee off the south side for the kitchen and related functions. It was on the east side of the river and paralleled Highway 10 with a setback of about 250 feet, leaving a large field in front for baseball and other games. The basement floor was half exposed, allowing each basement room to have windows, effectively making the main building four stories high. The main building housed most of the staff (about 15), all of the students (100 or so) and all of the classrooms. The staff lived in small private rooms located throughout the building and near to the students' dormitories.

Let's take an imaginary walk through the building starting on the top floor.

On the west end of the building were two boys' dormitories. A very large room running the full width of the building was immediately east. It was called the sewing room and was used for parties, sewing classes and many other things. Immediately to the east of the sewing room was an exciting room containing all of the things donated to the school by generous church members -- toys and games as well as clothing and shoes. Toys, games and new clothing were distributed at Christmas time. Used clothing was the rule at other times. The Stucki family was also permitted to dip into the 'Missionary Barrel.' I attended my Junior Prom in a patched, tweed suit from the 'Barrel,' much to my date's consternation.

Across from this room was the first of several large rooms that served as dormitories for the older girls. The rest of the 'big girls" dormitories were on the east end of the building on the third floor. These rooms had dressers and other amenities not found in the dormitories for the boys and the younger girls. I have no idea why this differentiation was made.

The rooms on the third floor had small windows because of the presence of the eaves. The troughs for catching water from the eaves were about 24 inches wide and about 3 inches deep and were located directly under the windows. The troughs were a part of the building wall rather than devices hanging from the roof. I later learned that adventuresome boys sometimes exited from one of their third floor windows, crawled up over the roof and down to the troughs under the girl's windows on their end of the building. Presumably equally adventuresome girls opened their windows and let the boys into their rooms although I have no direct evidence that this happened.

One could descend to the second floor using an outside fire escape porch, but this was discouraged. We will proceed to the second floor using the central stairwell on the "girls' side." Immediately to the east of the stairwell was an employees' bathroom and east of that, another bathroom that served both employees' rooms and the 'girls' sick rooms' that occupied the rest of the east end of the second floor. These rooms were for the isolation of sick girls and sometimes for visitors.

Moving westward from the stairwell, we come to girls' locker rooms and additional girls' dormitories. These were for the smaller girls. At the end of the east wing of the building was a steel fire door separating the boys' wing from the girls'. Similar fire doors were located on each floor of the building and served to isolate the wings from each other in the event of fire. The fire doors were connected to a concrete stairwell that was alleged to be fireproof and capable of standing even if everything around it burned. At each end of the building there was also a steel external fire escape. Fortunately, we never had a fire so the system did not get tested.

On the other side of the fire door were boys' dormitories and locker rooms and a stairwell that served that side of the building. All stairwells were open from top to bottom, something no longer permitted for safety reasons. Such stairwells act like chimneys in case of fire. Also located on each floor in several places were fire hoses connected to large-bore water pipes.

As we descend the boys' staircase to the first floor we encounter two large classrooms on the west end of the building. The one on the south was for Kindergarten, first and second grade and the one on the north for third, fourth and fifth.

Immediately east of the stairs were doors leading into a dining room stretching the full width of the building and east to the fire door. One corner of the dining room contained a commercial dishwasher, cupboards for dishes and a serving counter. A door on the south wall led to a large kitchen. The floor of the dining room was tongue-and-grove maple placed on a concrete sub-floor. In the summer time when the humidity was high, the wooden floor buckled into huge undulations. Eventually, I covered the floor with linoleum, but that really didn't stop the buckling.

A south door and a pass-through led to the large kitchen. This kitchen was in the tee wing off the south side of the main building on the boys' side. The kitchen contained an industrial-sized stove fired with fuel oil. It also contained a small kerosene stove used to cook small meals. A shelf above the large stove held a pot of coffee from which Dad poured cups all day. The coffee changed from hot to lukewarm to cold as the day went on, but he didn't mind.

The kitchen also had counters, a large kettle pressure cooker, an industrial-sized icebox, a food pantry and a utensils pantry. Ice was delivered to the icebox through a door opening to the outside that could be reached from the back of the ice truck. A large double sink was at the south end of the kitchen. Two porches, one on the east and one on the south were connected to the kitchen and to stairs that allowed entrance to the kitchen from the street level. In later years, the south porch was converted to a walk-in refrigerator/freezer and the icebox was retired.

Two floors were located above the kitchen and one floor below. The floors above the kitchen were for the cook's room and bath and the boys' sickrooms. A small spiral staircase right off of the kitchen led to the floors above and below.

The room below the kitchen was the "peeling room." It had long tables in it and an industrial sink. This was where the students so assigned would prepare vegetables for cooking. A boiler was also located here for heating the pressure cooker upstairs. Sometime in the 40's Dad bought a machine that peeled potatoes and other vegetables by whirling them in a tub lined with abrasive material. If you left potatoes in the machine too long, you had nothing left but 'small potatoes.'

If we return to the dinning room and exit it on the east, we find ourselves in the building's entry hall. Immediately off this hall is the superintendent's offices, an "outer" and an "inner." Across from these offices is the employees' lounge and further east, an employee's bedroom. Immediately behind the "inner" office and connected to it is a medical dispensary. Further down the hall is the girls' staircase and across from the staircase, on the north side, is a library. East of the library is a large classroom for the fifth through eighth grades. This room was also used for church services, for Friday night movies and for other functions attended by all students and staff.

If we go down in the basement using the girls' staircase and move east, the first room we see on the right is the girls' bathroom. On the left is the laundry room. It contained a large, rolling drum washer, an extractor, a mangle and a dryer. This was all industrial equipment. The dryer was particularly interesting. It consisted of a large, metal-clad room into which racks could be rolled. The racks would be draped with the clothes to be dried. After the doors of the dryer were closed, the hot water radiators inside and the fan were turned on. An hour or so later, the clothes were dry. This device was also used to dry corn and other vegetables in the summer time. The produce was spread out on trays loaded onto the racks.

Down the hall from the laundry room was a room used to store squash and other vegetables that could not stand the temperature of the Manual Training basement. It was also used to store preserved eggs. I never ate preserved eggs and have no idea how they were prepared.

West of the staircase on the south side of the hall was a large girls' playroom. Across from the playroom was the "tool room." It supposedly contained all the tools that were required to maintain the building and many other things. The school had an intercom system with convenient phones located on every floor. If an employee (only employees were allowed to use the intercom) wanted to make a call, he or she pushed the button to send an audible signal throughout the building. The employee whose signal was broadcast was to pick up a phone and answer. This intercom system was powered by a set of car batteries perpetually hooked up to a battery charger in the tool room. The whole thing exuded fumes and corrosion, but it kept the intercom going. One time I dreamed that I heard a phone buzz, looked up and saw the head of my 4th grade teacher, Miss Nelda Docken, emerging from the mouthpiece. Such is the material of nightmares.

The tool room included a huge vice attached to the workbench. During one idiotic episode, Pink Van Gordon and I squeezed .22 caliber blanks with the vice and then set them off by hitting the vice with a large hammer. After one blank lacerated Pink's thumb, we ceased this nonsense. It's lucky we didn't do greater damage to ourselves. This was one of my many summer adventures.

The grocery pantry was down the hall from the tool room. It held all of the grocery supplies that we bought from the Kickbush Grocery Company. The salesman would appear every two weeks and Dad would place the order for delivery the following week. Things such as coffee, flour, sugar, canned juices and other things we ourselves could not grow or produce were purchased. I remember going into this room, taking a large can of grapefruit juice and drinking it all by myself. This was in the summer, of course.

Down the hall from the pantry was the canned goods storage room where we kept the things we ourselves canned. This room was right next to the 'peeling room.'

The boiler room and the associated facilities were next. The boiler deserves a special mention. The main building was heated with steam or hot water (I can't remember which) piped through the building into banging radiators. The boiler was a behemoth covered with a thick layer of asbestos. It was located in a pit directly under the dining room on the first floor. A smaller boiler, also in the pit, provided hot water for cooking, laundry and bathing. Hot water or steam pipes throughout the building were shrouded with asbestos to keep the heat in until the hot water reached the radiators. We played in the boiler room often amid the asbestos flakes that fell from the disintegrating covering of the boilers. The point of this observation is that, to the best of my knowledge, none of us developed cancer from the asbestos. My conclusion is that the threat of asbestos, like many other modern threats, may be vastly overblown. It is tragic that the country paid so much for asbestos ablation that could have been spent on education.

The boilers (and the kitchen stove) were fired with a kind of crude oil; thick, gooey stuff that got very viscous in the cold. It was stored in tanks located under the front driveway of the main building. The oil was shipped to Neillsville by tank car. The car was stored on a siding in the railroad yard and oil was transported to the storage tanks at the school via a homemade flat tank that was placed on top of the school truck, an all-purpose Chevy ton-and-a-half flat-bed that served for everything from transporting the oil to transporting Indian children to town for a rare shopping spree. Transporting the oil was a messy business. Inevitably the truck, the tank, and the front driveway were all stained with oil spots that had a tendency to persist.

After the tank had been removed, the truck cleaned and truck racks put back in place, the truck could be used for other things including transporting children. We all stood up in the back and hung on to the racks. No seat belts were in evidence. When we were driven through town we would whoop and holler. Invariably, someone would say, "Let's be quiet. They might think we're Indians." While we thought this was funny, in retrospect, I think this really was evidence of self-loathing produced by the white man's effort to erase Indian culture.

The truck was also used to transport packages from the Post Office to the school. Particularly at Christmas time, churches would send clothing and toys to the school. One time my father, in an effort to make a movie that he could use to illustrate the welcome receipt of goods from the churches, filmed my uncles taking huge boxes off the truck and moving them into the school. The only trouble with the movie was that the boxes used in the movie were empty and this was obvious from the way they were handled. Retakes were rare in those days and the ridiculous scene was used again and again in churches all over the United States.

Further on down the hall were the boys' bathrooms and playroom. Both were subject to continual abuse for various reasons. One of the valued possessions of youth back then was the steel marble or 'steelie.' This was a ball bearing from a bearing race found in heavy machinery. After we had acquired a bearing race from the scrap yard by the machine shed, we had to break it open to get out the bearings. Many boys attempted to break the bearing races by pounding them on the corners of the porcelain urinals. The urinals got the worst of the deal. Plumbing fixtures were constantly being replaced or shored up with concrete.

The playrooms were just long rooms with benches on the sides. While there were basketball hoops in the playrooms, the ceilings were not high enough to make the game possible. Mostly playrooms were just places where the kids hung out and changed into or out of their outdoor winter clothing. The floors were cold concrete. One summer when I was in college, I tiled the playroom floors with ½-inch thick asbestos tile to make them more kid-friendly.

Let's return to the 'outer' office on the first floor. Immediately inside the office door on the right was a panel of buttons. Each button rang bells in a different region of the building and in the play areas outside. I think there may have been a dozen or so buttons. Bells were used to communicate with the students – when to get up, when to go to bed, when to eat, class time and playtime. Communication was quite primitive -- mostly bells and the aforementioned intercom. The whole school and our family had only one telephone line and two phones for communication with the outside world. One phone was located in the 'outer' office and one was located in our home. The number of rings determined who would answer. The school rated one ring and our house two. If someone at our house wished to call the office, he simply picked up the receiver and asked the operator to ring one. To call the house from the office, we asked the operator to ring two. We knew all the operators by name and they knew us. Our number was 232, ring one or two. There was only one 'exchange' in Neillsville and we had no area codes. Long distance calling was a major project and something rarely done.

I do recall one tragic long distance call. One evening one of the employees (Miss Docken?, Miss Wepner?) was called to the phone for an urgent message. Since there was little privacy in using the phone, several of us heard the anguished wail that emerged when she found out that her brother had just been shot and killed in a holdup. Apparently he and his friends were playing cards when the holdup man appeared with a gun and a demand that the card players put all their valuables on the table. Her brother tried to be a hero and kick the gun out of the robber's hand. His kick missed and he was shot dead. The robber was eventually caught and the incident became the cover story of a crime magazine that I believe was called, "Calling All Cars."

Play areas outside the building included some large swing sets, tetter-totters, giant strides, a big merry-go-round, sand boxes, a slide and a chinning bar. Dad was quite short and stocky. Most of his weight was in his upper body so he was an excellent "chinner" and would demonstrate his strength from time to time for us. Nobody could do as many chin-ups as he did. For those of you unfamiliar with old playground equipment, a giant stride is simply a high steel pole set in the ground. The pole is topped with a rotating disk to which long ropes are attached. The player grabs a rope and runs around the pole. Centrifugal force throws the player out into the air. As the force is dissipated, the player returns to the ground and pushes off again. Between each push-off and return is what was called a giant stride!

Chapter III – School Days

The Indian children began to arrive at the School in early September just as the Evergreen corn was becoming ready to eat. Most students were brought to the school by their parents or grandparents. Most lived within a day's drive but some came from greater distances. The large driveway and parking area in front of the school began to fill up with dilapidated cars shortly after the official day of annual enrollment. This was a very exciting time for the Stucki children as well as for the Indian children. Enrollment day was a time to renew friendships.

My best friend was Roy Garvin. In the summertime he lived with his parents in the woods about 15 miles from Neillsville. Sometimes I visited him at his home and was always treated to "cha" made in a special way by Mrs. Garvin. Cha is the Winnebago word for venison. She would sear small pieces of cha in bacon grease in a big iron pan together with slices of onion. Then she would pour water on the seared meat and onions for braising until the meat was very tender. This was served on boiled potatoes for the most delicious meal imaginable. The Garvins had fresh cha at all times of the year. I think this was the only meat they ever had. Their vegetables and potatoes were grown in a garden along side their house. In the summertime they picked blueberries and blackberries to eat, to dry and to sell.

A buyer would come to the Old Mission every few days to buy the berries from the Indians. He was a horrible little man. Apparently blind and very profane, he would shout and cajole the Indians into putting their berries into his truck. Then he would pay them with paper money that he carried in his hand. He always knew how many bills of each denomination he held and rarely if ever made a mistake in either paying or giving change. Sometimes I thought that maybe his blindness was an act. As far as I know, he did not cheat the Indians. I think one of his friends drove his truck.

When Roy and his parents arrived at the school it was time to discuss what had gone on all summer. One time we were talking about these things in the back seat of his Dad's car. While we were fooling around as kids will do, I upset a coffee can filled with a brown liquid that Roy explained was tobacco juice.

The parents enrolled their children and made sure that all belongings were recorded. This was done in Dad's office. The parents and their children were then shown their beds by other employees and to the other places where the children would be spending the next nine months, and were fed a delicious meal or two in the dining room. That evening or perhaps the next day the parents drove home. Before leaving many gave their children little going away gifts. Often the gift was box of fry bread or 'wy-scup-da-hede' as they called it. Occasionally it was something a little less benign, like peyote. Many of the parents subscribed to the peyote tradition and wanted to be sure that their children were not deprived of the sacrament while at school. Dad routinely confiscated the peyote if he found it.

That these parents sent their children to school was a testament to their belief in the value of education. A little over a half century before, the Winnebago Indians living on the sand near Black River Falls had hired a schoolmaster to teach their children how to read and write, realizing that this was the only way they could survive in a white-dominated world. The school failed but was replaced by the Old Mission School in 1878.

Soon after the students were enrolled, the state of health of each was determined. Of particular concern were tuberculosis and trachoma. Trachoma is an infectious disease of the eye caused by the microorganism, *Chlamydia trachomatis.* The disease is very common in third world environments today and is among the leading causes of blindness. In the 1930s trachoma was common among the Winnebago children. The treatment in those days was surgical. The disease affects the eyelid causing scaring and a turning in of the eyelid and eyelashes. The scarring and the turned-in eyelashes lacerate the cornea. Children with trachoma underwent an operation called eyelid scraping, a procedure that involved the removal of the offending tissue with a scraper. After all of the infected children were identified, a government doctor arrived at the school and one by one their eyelids were scraped on the operating table in the dispensary. The effect of the surgery lasted about a year, as I recall, so there were many repeat infections each year. One of the customary greetings between children at the beginning of the school year was, "Did you get scraped yet?" In those days we lacked antibiotics. The treatment today is an antibiotic ointment, generally tetracycline, and careful attention to hygiene.

In a few days the kids were all settled down to their school routines. Unlike students in modern boarding schools, our students were expected to do chores as well as attend classes. The boys and girls were organized into groups called boys number one, boys number two, girls number one and girls number two. At the end of each meal the principal would announce which group would clear and wash, and which would dry and set tables for the next meal. There would be a closing song, stools would scrape back from the tables and the din of dishwashing would begin. The 100 or so students sat at oblong tables on stools and ate from aluminum plates and drank from aluminum cups. These utensils made a great deal of noise when handled roughly. The dishes were washed in the large industrial dishwasher and dried by hand with towels. The whole task was completed in a short time because only after it was finished could the assigned students go out and play.

Students were also assigned tasks like sweeping, kitchen duty, farm duty, mending and the like. Today, there are prohibitions against such assignments because of the fear that institutions might exploit the children. In our day, such assignments were regarded as an essential part of a child's education. Institutionalized children today live in a very boring, sterile and artificial environment in my opinion. We were seldom bored and we all learned many life skills.

The Stucki children all had their own chores at home. Mine included cleaning out the ash pit in our wood-fired cooking stove, keeping the wood box filled with wood, and fetching the milk from the milk house. I would take a 6-quart aluminum pail with a tight cover down to the milk house, open a 20-gallon can of milk, stir the milk with the slotted stirring tool to be certain that cream was evenly distributed, and dip out the milk with a long-handled dipper. Careful attention to keeping dirt out of the milk and to washing the utensils in the spring water was required. Then came the trip up the hill with the now heavy bucket. The discovery that carrying two cans each half-filled with milk was easier than carrying only one full can was independently made.

About 50 feet to the west of the springhouse was a place where we burned our trash and butchered chickens. Trash burning and chicken butchering were also on my list of chores. It never occurred to me that chicken rearing, chicken butchering and trash burning might be something that ought to be kept far away from a spring. But then again, the springhouse did not seem to be situated so that any kind of runoff from either endeavor would occur.

Chicken butchering required a log and a hatchet, both of which we kept nearby. I was quite handy with the hatchet and could decapitate a bird with one carefully aimed blow. The choice then was to hold the struggling bird as it shook and bled or to toss it on the ground and let it flop. The choice was a toss-up, no pun intended. If I held the chicken until it bled out, I got blood all over my pants. If I tossed the decapitated chicken to the ground, it got all covered with blood as it flopped around, making it harder to pluck.

After the bleeding was over, the chicken was dipped into a pail of very hot water brought down from our house and the wet feathers were plucked. The feathers were tossed on the ash pile to be incinerated the next time a junk fire was required. The smell of burning feathers is one never to be forgotten. The birds were eviscerated in the kitchen and the offal fed to the hogs. I think we had chicken about once a week. My appetite for chicken remains very healthy to this day. "A chicken in every pot" was more than just a political slogan. It was a way of life for us.

The classroom situation was a little like what one might find in any small school. We had three schoolrooms, each with three grades. One teacher for each room taught all three classes in turn. From my point of view this was a terrific way to go. Because the Stucki children had had the luxury of learning how to read, write and count at home before entering school, many times we found ourselves rather impatient with the instruction given to our particular grade. However, we could always listen to the lessons being given to the next higher grade if we were in a lower class. Of course, this only compounded the problem because that meant that we would become impatient when we graduated to the grade we had been listening in on. Dad and my teachers took care of that problem to some extent when they promoted me by two grades rather than one when I was leaving, I believe, fifth grade. I must admit that the ease with which my siblings and I met the challenges of school sometimes led us into mischief.

When sister Peg was in sixth grade and I was in seventh, Miss Kippenhan (Kippy), who was both our teacher and the school principal, stepped out of the room. Peg had some nuts in her pocket and proceeded to take one out and crack it on the floor with the heel of her shoe much like Khrushchev at the UN. She didn't hear Miss Kippenhan return to the classroom and did not become aware of her until she saw Kippy's shoes, and looked up at her glowering face. The rest of the students had seen the whole display. Peg missed it all, laughing manically as she banged away at the nut. We all thought it was very funny. Kippy did not admit to the humor of the situation until many years later.

Another one of the chores assigned to the boys was the airing and brushing of the clothing sent to the school for the missionary barrel. When I was in eighth grade one of my classmates passed around some pictures he had found in the pocket of a coat he was brushing. The pictures were a series of eight amateur shots of a couple engaging in sex, not just ordinary sex but the kind of sex that until recently was never mentioned in polite or even impolite society. The pictures made it up and down the aisles, but were carefully kept away from the girls.

Not all of the lessons took place in the formal classroom. The boys all took Manual Training and farming and the girls all took home economics consisting of sewing, mending, cooking, cleaning, and baby care. Mom taught many of these classes in addition to raising her own brood of seven. Like Dad, Mom was a remarkable person.

Manual Training produced some humorous moments for me. Our teacher was a man who came in just one day a week for our class. He was not terribly bright as I recall. One day our assignment was to make a hammer handle with a drawshave. A drawshave is a kind of knife that you pull toward you against a piece of wood held tightly in a vise for the purpose of shaping the wood by cutting off thin strips in a controlled manner. Each of us was given a single piece of 2-inch x 2-inch wood about 12 inches long, a drawshave and a bench with a vise. I immediately discovered that my piece of wood contained a large knot that precluded any kind of orderly shaping of the piece. But teacher ignored me when I asked for a better piece of wood. So I shrugged and went to work with my drawshave. After a bit I had produced a mangled piece of kindling wood that didn't even remotely resemble a hammer handle. At the end of the period we were told to offer the results of our work for grading. When teacher came to me, he solemnly took the wood and turned it around in his hand very carefully, examining it from all sides, and then proclaimed that I had earned an F for my effort. I took back the stick and could barely conceal my contempt. Any idiot could see with one glance that I had failed and why I had failed. The solemn examination of my work just cracked me up. I remember thinking, "What a stupid jerk this guy is."

Another time we had to build a device for making rope out of binder twine and then make a length of rope. We worked in groups since making rope took more than one person. In the Manual Training classroom was a shop stove, opening on the top. It was used to burn scrap and keep the room warm. After we had completed twisting our rope we were told to pass it rapidly through the fire in the stove to singe off the excess "hair" on the rope. I guess we didn't pass ours rapidly enough. The entire rope burned to a crisp before we could rescue it. Another F!

Farming at the Indian School had two purposes. One was to provide a means to teach students (male) the elements of farming for future application. The other was to provide products for use at the school. The farm provided vegetables, eggs and chickens, beef and pork, milk, mutton, wool, firewood and some grains. While we were learning how to farm, we were also contributing valuable labor to the effort. A word about the mutton is in order. During the Depression, the school was given truckload after truckload of sheep by the government. The sheep were sheared for the wool. Most were ultimately butchered for meat. I hated mutton and rejoiced whenever the last sheep in the field was dispatched. Shortly afterward, another truckload of sheep appeared and the process started all over again. It was many years before I was able to enjoy lamb. I still don't willingly eat mutton.

The first thing we did in the fall was to fill the silo with corn silage. We took teams of horses and flat wagons out into the cornfields; then as we cut down the corn stalks by hand, we loaded the stalks onto the wagon in an orderly fashion, with the butt end of each stalk oriented to the same side of the wagon. The filled wagons were driven to the barnyard and pulled up alongside the silage chopper. The chopper was located near the silo and was connected to a conveyer trough in which a flat chain with baffles ran. As the chopper delivered silage to the trough, the chain drive moved the silage up to the top of the silo, where each little clump of silage was dumped into the silo. In later years we were to acquire a device that delivered the silage by a blower, but what I remember most was the conveyer chain. Single-cylinder gasoline engines made, I believe, by John Deere, powered all these devices. The engines were connected to the machines by belt drives.

A team of students unloaded the cornstalks onto the apron of the chopper while another student fed the stalks, butt end first, into the chopper. This was very dangerous work. Extreme care was taken to avoid getting ones hands pulled into the chopper. Other students were assigned to work inside the silo. The conveyer dumped all of the silage in one spot. The silage had to be spread around evenly and tramped down carefully so it would ferment properly. Later on when we had the blower, we simply distributed the silage evenly by moving the nozzle of the blower.

One time I was assigned duty inside the silo and in the process of working, lost my classic, Ingersoll, one-dollar pocket watch. It was a rugged watch with a hard plastic face cover, but no metal snap cover over the front of the watch. It was attached to a small watch fob. I despaired of ever seeing that watch again, but several months later I found it in a feeding trough. Apparently it had survived the silage fermentation process and was shoveled into the feeding trough together with the ration of silage. The cows had chewed on my watch a bit, but otherwise it was intact. I opened the back of the watch, dipped the entire thing in a bucket of kerosene, shook it dry, snapped the back cover shut and wound it up. It started ticking and keeping time again as if nothing had happened.

Milking and otherwise taking care of the cows was something else we learned. The milking was done by hand the old-fashioned way. You approach the cow from the right rear, put your hand on the back of the cow to show her you are there to clean her udder and milk her. You sit on a milk stool. If you are skilled, you sit on a one-legged stool. You hold the bucket between you knees and begin to squeeze the teats rhythmically. If you know what you are doing, and the cow knows what you are doing, she "lets down her milk." This is a well-known pituitary neuro-endocrine driven response. Often times when human mothers see that their babes are hungry, they spontaneously let down their milk, sometimes to their embarrassment. Their milk often copiously flows out of their nipples and stains their clothing before they can get the babe to the breast.

After the cow has been milked and 'stripped' to get the last of the milk out of the udder, the milk was weighed and taken to the 20-gallon milk can topped by a funnel with a replaceable filter. When the milk was poured through the filter you could see how much chaff and other contamination was in the milk. When full, the can was covered and placed in the cool milk house. The milk received no other treatment before it was consumed. Of course we always had our cows tested for Bang's disease and tuberculosis. As an aside, I must say that un-pasteurized milk does taste better than the pasteurized stuff, but I would never drink un-pasteurized milk today. Despite the improvements in milking techniques, the long supply chain for milk would make drinking un-pasteurized milk risky.

The school farm was proud of its cattle and tried to keep milk and butterfat production high by proper feeding and breeding. Butterfat content was measured periodically using the Babcock Test invented at the University of Wisconsin School of Agriculture. All of us learned how to conduct the test. As I recall, it was performed as follows: a measured amount of well-mixed milk was placed in a flask with a long, graduated neck. Several milliliters of pure sulfuric acid were added using a pipette. The acid had to be gradually eased into the milk so there was no sputtering. If milk is added to the acid rather than acid to milk, there is a large exothermic reaction that causes the whole thing to literally explode and throw acid all about. We all learned the hard way that sulfuric acid burns can be very painful.

The flask full of milk and acid is mixed thoroughly by putting a cover on the top and inverting it several times. The whole flask becomes very warm as the acid/milk reaction takes place. Apparently the acid denatures the milk protein and causes it to release the butterfat. The flask is then placed in a hand-cranked centrifuge and spun for several minutes. When the flask is removed, there is a clear band of yellow oil in the neck of the flask. The length of this band is measured against a scale that reads as a percentage of butterfat. For a Holstein cow, a butterfat level of 4% or higher was good. A periodic measurement of butterfat was made for each cow in the herd. When a cow got too old and its milk and butterfat production went down, it was butchered.

A cow will produce milk for only a certain period of time after having a calf. Therefore, it is necessary to breed each milk cow periodically to cause it to 'freshen.' We generally did not keep a bull for breeding purposes because bulls can be very dangerous and are non-productive except when used for breeding. We relied on a neighbor's bull. When a cow came into heat, something we could ascertain by the cow's mounting behavior, we called for the bull. It was generally led or trucked over to our farm and introduced to the cow. Naturally, we all expressed great interest in the breeding process and had many sophomoric jokes about breeding to pass around.

In those days there was no such thing as artificial insemination so it was difficult to develop a good herd of milk cows without a quality bull. Most of the farmers in our territory did not have enough money to have high quality bulls, so the breeding effort concentrated on the performance of the dam rather than the sire. Today it is much easier to breed outstanding herds using artificial insemination.

We were also taught how to butcher hogs and chickens. I don't remember ever learning how to butcher a cow at the Indian School; I learned that in Grandpa Kuester's butcher shop. Our hog-butchering lesson is one I will never forget. The process required the heating of perhaps 50 gallons of water in a large iron kettle built into a brick stove in the slaughterhouse. A fire of wooden logs was ignited in the stove and when the water was hot, the chosen hog was herded into the slaughterhouse from the pigpen and the door was closed. The hog was to be killed by a shot to the brain from a .22-caliber rifle. Our farm manager and farming teacher at that time was Mark Vornholt, a dour would-be minister who rarely smiled.

Instead of shooting the hog himself, Mark handed the gun to one of the students, told him to aim between the eyes and pull the trigger. About ten of us were standing around observing. The student with the gun took careful aim but waited while the hog slowly moved toward him. Mark said, "Shoot, shoot," but the student waited until the hog was directly in front of him before he pulled the trigger. He hit the hog right between the eyes, but since the angle of the shot was inappropriate, the bullet traveled down through the roof of the hog's mouth rather than through the brain. The hog squealed loudly and began running around the room. Mark said, "Give me that gun!," and when he had it he began firing at the running hog. Amazingly enough he didn't hit any of the students and finally brought down the hog.

The dead hog was then hoisted up in the air with a special hoist, was bled out through a cut in the neck and dipped into the boiling water for a few minutes. It was then brought out and placed, with the hoist, on a large table. The dipping had the effect of loosening the hair and the outer layer of the skin. Both could then be scraped off the hog with special scrapers. We all helped with that task.

After the hog was clean, it was again hoisted into the air and opened up from chin to anus. The guts, the lungs and liver, heart and everything else were removed. After the liver and heart and sometimes other useful things were salvaged, the rest of the offal was put into a tub and dumped into the pigpen where it was eaten by the other pigs. Nothing went to waste.

After the carcass had cooled, it was cut up into the various parts so familiar to all of us, even today – bacon, hams, loins, shoulders, spare ribs and copious quantities of fat to be rendered into lard in the big dipping kettle at a future date. I think we did have a smoke house at the school, but I can't recall where it was. The handling of the meat after it was cut into the appropriate parts was the responsibility of the females, not the males. Butchering was done when the weather was cold so the problem of refrigeration was minimal.

Mark also taught us how to castrate boars or at least he demonstrated the technique. I remember that demonstration very well. The boar was huge and much too old for a routine castration, but Mark went ahead anyway. First he forced the boar on its back using ropes to pull its legs out from under.

Then he asked four boys to hold the legs and he knelt astride the beast's belly and with his knife cut into the scrotum in two places. After he had extracted the testicles by simply pulling on them, he attempted to get up. I think the boys holding the hind legs figured it was time to let go and they did. The animal started squealing and kicking. Its hind legs caught hold of the crotch of Mark's overalls and ripped them to shreds. While the boar exposed Mark's testicles in the process of ripping his pants, he did them no harm – fortunately.

Another lesson/chore was the harvesting of the ripe field corn. We used a bin wagon with a bang-board for that job. The wagon was pulled through the cornfield by the horses. The pickers would walk along the rows, break off the ripe ears and toss them toward the band-board. The cobs were supposed to hit the board and drop into the wagon. Later on we shucked the corn using a tool with a sharp prong that was worn on the right hand like a short glove. Shucking was often done in the evening with boys and girls sitting in a circle around a pile of cobs on the ground. The lucky boy who found a red ear could (or was required to) kiss one of the girls.

The corn was used either on the ear for the hogs or was shelled for chickens and for grinding using another hand-powered tool. The shelling tool was a rotating disk with surface knobs. The corncobs were fed into a funnel one at a time and the handle was turned. The rotating disk knocked the kernels off the cob.

We had another machine with a rotating disk and a hand crank. This machine was kept in front of the cows and was used to chop up 'mangles' (as we called sugar beets back then). The chopped mangles were fed to the cows. It seemed to me that the flesh of those sugar beets was not very sweet. Maybe they were a special strain with much protein and little sugar content.

All was not chores and schooling. As the days grew shorter, twilight hours were spent playing kick-the-can or no-touching-the-ground tag. Kick-the-can went something like this: an empty tomato can was placed on the crest of the hill leading down to the river. The person who was 'it' kicked the can down the hill and then went to retrieve it. Meanwhile, everyone else hid. When the 'it' guy got back up to the crest of the hill, he put down the can and began to search for the hiders. The hiders would try to sneak out to the can and kick it down the hill again. If they succeeded, the 'it' guy went after the can again. If the 'it' guy found a hider, he would call out the name of the hider and race him to the can. If the 'it' guy succeeded in kicking the can down the hill before the located hider could get to it, that hider was now 'it.' The game had no obvious end, only a beginning. Darkness usually ended the game.

Fall was also the time when the butternuts began to ripen. We all loved butternuts and began to harvest them even before they were ripe. The trick was to get a stick of wood and throw it up into the trees to knock the nuts off the branches. After collecting the green nuts, we would crack them with a stone and extract the delicious meat for immediate consumption. We often cracked the nuts on the wide, concrete banisters of the steps leading up to the various back entrances of the school. Repeated use of the same places would wear depressions in the concrete, making it very easy to stand the nut upright for the coup de grace. Green butternut juice stains everything it touches a deep brown. Indeed, the Indian used butternut juice as a natural dye. A dark brown hand was clear evidence that one had found and eaten many nuts.

Fall was also the time for harvesting many other foods, including the much-loved Evergreen Sweet corn. Kids would carry cobs of corn away from the tables in the dining room for later consumption. The corncobs also made nifty missiles for a variety of war games.

Tomatoes were grown here by the ton. Before the first hard frost, the still green tomatoes were put on huge piles in the fields and covered with tarpaper. The tarpaper was removed during the warm fall days and as the tomatoes ripened they were retrieved for processing. Of course, the early ripening tomatoes had already been picked from the vine and processed. In our case, processing involved peeling the tomatoes and canning them either as stewed tomatoes or as tomato jam. Most people have never heard of tomato jam, but for us it was a staple. Tomato jam is made with sugar and pectin and tastes heavenly, as I remember. It was served to the Indian children at virtually every meal. Tomato jam was put up in glass jars. Stewed tomatoes were put up in tin cans.

The school had a hand-cranked can-sealing machine and a large pressure cooker for cooking and sterilizing the cans and their contents after filling. Both devices were hand built by Dad. The pressure cooker was heated with steam produced by a small boiler in the 'peeling room.' The filled and sterilized cans of tomatoes, beans, corn and peas were stored in a dark room immediately off the 'peeling room.' Our quality control was perhaps not what it should be so occasionally we would hear a loud pop as a fermenting can exploded or the cook or her helpers would find bulged 'leakers' when they went to retrieve cans for the next meal. As far as I know, no one ever suffered from food poisoning as a result of our poor quality control.

Cans were opened with a special opener that cut off the tops. This allowed the reuse of each can for a number of times after the can had been re-flanged. Re-flanging was done with the sealing machine using an attachment differing somewhat from the one used for sealing. Cans were placed on the turntable and the crank was turned. The attachment engaged the can as it was turning and gradually the new flange would appear. It took about twenty turns of the handle to re-flange one can. It got to be rather boring to turn the handle only, so once when I was re-flanging cans, I set up a production line where I would move cans into position with my left hand while cranking with my right. Inadvertently, I moved an un-re-flanged can to the back of the machine while I was cranking, and my right thumb came down hard on its sharp edge. It penetrated my thumb to the extent that when I withdrew my hand the can came with it. I think it penetrated the thumb bone. In any event, it hurt like hell.

Fall was also a time for 'jumping rocks' in the river. At that time of year the river was generally low and could be crossed in many places simply by jumping from one rock to the next. The idea was to get across the river, a distance of about a hundred yards, and return without getting wet feet. A slippery rock could land you in the water at best or break your arm at worst.

As the days got shorter, we turned our attention to repairing the bobsleds stored in the Manual Training building. These sleds were made by hand and consisted of a long board to which was attached a semi-fixed, double-runner rear element. This element was bolted to the board through a rounded block of wood that permitted the rear element to rock. A single bolt attached the front double runner. A rope loop was attached to the front of that runner for steering. A foot brace on the front of the board completed the sled. The driver sat in front, put his feet on the foot brace and held the rope loop on the outsides of his boots. The sled was steered by pulling on either side of the loop. Passengers sat behind the driver. A strip of metal attached with screws covered the bottom of each runner. The idea was to make the runner slippery so it would go faster on the snow and ice. This required much polishing and honing of the metal strip. The sleds ranged in size from eight feet long to about three feet long. The smallest sled was the property of Herbert Lone Tree. Most other sleds were regarded as community property.

We also made barrel staves in Manual Training. This involved taking an old barrel apart, preferably the kind with staves about ¼ inch thick. The stave was then polished and waxed and a piece of hardware cloth was fastened to the concave side of the stave to give the feet a grip. The thing was ridden with two feet on the stave, one behind the other. Arms were extended to the sides for balance as the stave was ridden down the hill.

After a few days of really cold weather, the ice on the river was frozen enough to permit skating. On a day of his choice, Dad would proceed to the river with an axe and test the depth and strength of the ice in several places. He would also mark areas that should be avoided like the area where the septic tanks discharged. After Dad pronounced the river safe, we could all go skating. We used shared clamp-on skates that we attached to our school shoes.

Wintertime was almost synonymous with Christmas time. Much effort went into making this a very significant holiday, not surprising at a Christian school. In addition to Christmas trees and presents from the Missionary Barrel, there was a large, lighted silver star that was hung every year on the gable atop the main entrance to the main building.

The most notable thing about the Christmas Season was the Annual Christmas Pageant! It was put on at the school for the school children, their parents and the staff in the combined two lower classrooms. A wall that could be folded away separated these classrooms. One year we also performed the Pageant for the townspeople in the Neillsville Armory. This was a really big deal for all of us.

Students were assigned different parts and Dad was always the cruel Caesar Augustus who said, "I know what I'll do, I know what I'll do, and I'll do it, I'll do it." He was referring to his decision to kill all the baby boys in the area to assure the death of the newborn Jesus. He then called his Centurion and told him to "Chose the hardest men in your command, men who would not shrink from a task so dastardly...etc. etc." Dad wrote the play and probably created that part for himself so that he could show off his considerable acting and emoting skill.

I often had the part of a shepherd, but never a Wise Man because I was too small. Most of my classmates were older than I and, of course, taller and heavier. Wise Men had to be at least 6 feet tall. In one scene, several of us shepherds stood around a "campfire" built on a hidden wooden platform surrounded by rocks. The fire consisted of some partly charred logs stacked up in a teepee shape with a concealed light, burning punk for smoke and a tiny electric fan to make some attached colored shreds of paper flutter. It was an altogether impressive and realistic fire. Dad had designed it and put it together. It was retained from year to year in the costume storeroom.

As shepherds standing or sitting around the fire, leaning on our crooks, we had to remark on the weather, the fact that it had been "…. a dark night and exceeding cold." "Aye, 'twas a weary task to gather all our sheep." "Think ye none were left behind?" The rumor that there had been a strange star in the sky foretelling the coming of the Messiah was discussed. Finally one of the shepherds said, "Hark! Me thinks me hears the howling of the wolves!" Another said, "Come let us be gone," and we all roused ourselves and trouped off stage. Owing to the position on stage that I occupied, I was the last shepherd to exit.

On the night we performed for the Neillsville townspeople in the Neillsville Armory, as I exited the stage and the curtain was coming down, ever one to be helpful, and knowing that the next scene had a different set, I halted my exit. I turned around and picked up the "burning" fire by the top stick and carried it off while the curtain was still a good two feet off the surface of the stage. A roar of laughter and appreciation arose from the audience. This was my first, but by no means my last, theatrical gaffe.

Soon after Easter, also celebrated at the school each year, spring would arrive, the ice would go out of the river around March 15, and recreational and other activities changed. We again played on the merry-go-round, the swings and the giant strides. We climbed over the face of the cliff and poked around in the river looking for this and that.

Spring also brought baseball played on the field in front of the main building. As I noted before, I was smaller (and less skilled) than my classmates and also younger than even many of the kids several grades under me. But occasionally they did let me play baseball with them. One day as I slid into second base, Dad was walking by and from a considerable distance he yelled, "Safe." Now I knew, and the second baseman knew, that I was really 'out,' but what to do. Neither of us wanted to contradict Dad, so I was assumed to be "safe" and the game went on.

I have always wished that I had contradicted Dad and admitted that I was 'out.' I was ashamed of myself for being so 'chicken.' I am sure my companions regarded this as yet another instance of favoritism being shown toward the superintendent's children. The Stucki children faced this problem all the time. We were 'minorities' in our school, but we were privileged minorities. For example, while we attended school with the Indian kids and were treated the same by our teachers, we lived at home in greater comfort than the Indian kids. Our classmates were generally older than we were. I was the youngest in my eighth grade class. The oldest was 21. It must have been somewhat humiliating to the older children to be compared to a smart-mouthed kid. We also got to eat at the employees' table in the big dining room when we were invited down for Sunday dinner. The employees ate from china and had a white tablecloth. Employee dishes were washed by hand in the kitchen.

The resentment that privilege produced led to many instances of isolation, insult and even beatings. I don't recall ever complaining to Dad about these 'treatments'; probably for fear that complaint would lead to even more trouble. I think I developed some appreciation for how true minorities must feel in hostile situations. I remember trying to identify myself as 'Indian' when we went to town or found ourselves in the outside world with our classmates. This mixed self-perception did have some influence on my later behavior, I am sure.

****

With the exception of baseball, basketball and some football, the recreational activities were mostly of our own invention. If we needed something for an activity, we built it ourselves. As with most kids, activities came and went in waves.

For example, one of the "early adopters" (as they would be called today) would procure a wheel of some sort from the scrap yard. The best wheels would be simple hoops of steel. In those days, steel hoops were used to protect wheels of all sorts, including farm wagon wheels and the wheels of small implements. The ideal steel hoop would be six to fifteen inches in diameter and an inch wide. A stick with a crosspiece of wood about six inches long was fashioned and was used to start the hoop rolling and the keep it rolling with steady pressure from behind with the stick. The idea was to keep the thing going as long as possible and maneuver it around obstacle courses we constructed. Soon everybody had a hoop and a stick.

Spool-carts were another fad. These carts were made with thread spools and wire and could be made in a variety of ways. The simplest had a front wheel and a back wheel. Others had many wheels and looked like rolling caterpillars. Powered by gravity, the spool-carts would run down tracks constructed in the sandboxes or on the hills by the river.

Scooters were made with boards and old roller-skate or similar wheels from furniture. These wheels were also found in the scrap yard. A set of handles was fastened to the board. Since scooters were rather complicated, they were generally made in a manual training class.

Sword fighting was a favorite pastime. We all fancied ourselves to be Errol Flynn or maybe one of the Three Musketeers. We made our swords out of wooden lath strips (used to build plastered walls). They broke rather easily, but that may have been a good thing. We often used peach basket covers for shields. Sometimes we fought with small wooden daggers as well.

In the years before I attended the Indian School, basketball was very important and because so many of the boys were older, their teams played both high school and college teams. They practiced in the Neillsville High School gym or the Armory

****

In late May and early June it was time to go home for most Indian children. A few with no place to go were allowed to stay at the school through the summer. At that time they enjoyed most of the privileges of staff, including eating from china at a common table.

Chapter IV – Summer Time

Summertime for the Stucki family, for the few Indian children remaining at the school and for the school staff was quite a change from wintertime and the school year. Summer started out with the planting of the truck gardens. The gardener, my Uncle Jack, did this meticulous work for many years. Later when Uncle Jack left the school to become a lumberjack in northern Wisconsin, the gardening work was taken over by Mr. Hauser, the father of Gretchen Hauser, the middle grades teacher.

All summer long the truck gardens required care, and fruits and vegetables had to be harvested and processed at the appropriate time. Everyone helped with the work, even the teachers and matrons, and of course, the cooks. We kids had to help also, as did the Indian children who remained at the school. During the day, we would pick the beans, tomatoes, strawberries or corn -- whatever was ripe. In the evening we would sit out on the porch off the kitchen and snip and cut the beans or peel the tomatoes. The corn was cut off the cobs with a dangerous-looking device that required that the cob be held against the knives with the hand. Only the cook was allowed to use that tool.

Of course, while we sat and worked there was a lot of conversation. Most of it was good-natured banter, but sometimes it got nasty. I remember once when my sister, Marie teed off on me and greatly insulted my integrity, my intelligence, my appearance and everything else about me. I was greatly offended, but held my tongue.

Once when we were picking strawberries, there was a beautiful sunset. One of the teachers said to Miss Hartz, the cook, "Hartzy look at the beautiful sunset." Miss Hartz growled back, "I don't have time to look up." Often when Miss Hartz was not around one of us would growl her famous line for a good laugh by all. It should be said that

Miss Hartz suffered from plantar warts which caused her no end of pain. As far as I know, she never had the warts treated and suffered pretty much in silence, but it did make her grouchy.

****

Most of the Indian children returned to their homes for the summer, where they picked berries or manufactured crafts, particularly baskets and beadwork. Baskets were made out of white ash strips separated by soaking an ash log in water and pounding it with a rock. Beadwork was usually done on buckskin.

Indian crafts were often sold from roadside stands, but this was not a very effective marketing strategy, so in 1941 Dad and several of the Indians formed a Winnebago Handcraft Cooperative. Members of the Co-op made baskets and other things and brought everything to several sales points, one at the Old Mission and one at the Indian School. There may have been others as well. In addition to using advertising to move the product, the Co-op made contracts with various outlets to handle their products on consignment or made actual bulk sales to other organizations.

I remember one sale in particular. The contract was with a cheese company near Lodi, Wisconsin. The Co-op members were to make 1,500 round, covered baskets. Each would be filled with various cheeses and then placed in a cardboard carton for shipping to the consumer. I had the responsibility of driving the Indian School truck down to Lodi with a full load of baskets. The cheese company accepted the baskets but later there was complaining that led to recall of some of the baskets. Apparently, despite careful instructions as to dimensions, some of the baskets were either too small and could not hold the cheeses or were too large to fit in the shipping cartons. The rejects were returned and sold individually through the Co-op stores. Artistry does not lend itself well to mass production. Most of the basket makers were very proud of their output and almost always signed their work. I treasure several very fine pieces that I bought over the years. I don't think the Co-op ever solved the mass production problem.

In 1946 the Co-op built a small grocery store at the Old Mission where Indians could trade beadwork and baskets for groceries. At the Co-op Store, they could buy staples at less than they would cost after the seven-mile trip into town. One day the keys to the store were lost and Mom suggested that a certain Indian had taken them. I went to the Indian's house and rashly accused him of taking the keys. He denied having them. Then Mom found them where she has put them. I was very ashamed of myself for having made this false accusation.

In 1969 the Winnebago Handicraft Cooperative and co-op store went out of business. Individual Indian craft people continued to make and sell baskets and beadwork individually, but such craft work is becoming rare.

****

It was in the 1940's that a vicious tornado traveled through the city of Black River Falls. Mom and I were working at the Old Mission. From the Old Mission it looked like a wide, black column. It appeared to be standing still which was very bad news because that suggested it was coming straight toward us. We cowered in a ditch and soon the thing veered to the north and was out of sight. While we were watching it go through Black River Falls, we could see what looked like leaves whirling around. Since we were seven miles away, the 'leaves' could only have been large pieces of debris like detached roofs.

The tornado had headed northeast which was the direction of Neillsville and the Indian School. So Mom and I jumped into the truck and headed for home. From time to time we would see a devastated farm or woodlot but no people. We didn't stop to investigate anything because it was about an hour's drive to Neillsville. When we got to the Indian School, we were told that the tornado had just barely missed the school and its grounds but that it had completely destroyed a beautiful grove of white pines up by the railroad bridge. This had been a favorite grove for picnics and just playing around. No one was hurt at the Indian School.

After we told Dad what we had seen on the way back to Neillsville, he insisted that he and I get in the car and drive back toward the Old Mission to see if anyone along the way had been hurt. We found several homes and farms that had been utterly demolished, but there were no casualties. I remember one old woman we saw standing in the ruins of her home with a silver spoon in her hands. She wasn't saying anything, just rubbing her spoon. Dad told her to come to the Indian School at Neillsville if she needed anything. I don't know if she came or not.

****

One of the reasons I considered myself to be an adult by age 11 or 12 was that by then I was working almost full time during the summers on the Indian School farm. Earlier than that, I had worked part-time doing those things that the farmer thought I could manage.

From the time I was very small, I followed the school farmer, Adolph Gander, everywhere. I was bothering him no doubt, but I wanted to help him, and Gander (he always wanted to be called simply, Gander) patiently tolerated me. I learned how to slop hogs, call the cows, 'come bos, come bos,' feed the chickens and drive the team of horses. I helped gather the eggs from the nests and from the chicken yard. I vividly recall walking around in the chicken yard barefoot through the droppings and loose feathers. Fresh droppings oozed up between my toes like ribbon candy.

One day Gander got a bright idea. He said, "Let's make some spinach soup." This was in the early summer and I think the cook was on vacation, so we were supposed to make our own meals. So we picked some fine-looking spinach from the truck garden, brought it into the kitchen, washed it and chopped it up. We lit the kerosene stove in the big kitchen and put the spinach in a pot with some fresh milk and set it to boil. Then Gander threw in a handful of salt to season the soup. After some time, we tasted the soup. It was so salty that it was impossible to eat. We took it out and tried to feed it to the hogs. It was even too salty for them.

Gander had an unresolved hair-lip causing him to speak in a peculiar way. This did not bother us, but it did make for some memorable statements on his part. We were driving somewhere one hot summer day and stopped at a country store in Christie, Wisconsin for a beer for Gander and a cold pop for me. After taking a long pull on his bottle, Gander said, "Golly I like beer. I could drink beer until I busht," the last word being emphasized strongly.

When I was nine, Gander and his new wife, Bertha, took me with them to visit his ancestral home in Kentucky. I remember their car very well. It was a brand new 1935 Ford Coupe with a single front bench seat, no back seat, and a back window shelf for storage. When I tried to get into the car and sit between them on the front seat, Gander said, "No. Women sit in the middle and men sit on the outside." The outside seat it was, except when I wanted to sleep. Then it was the back shelf.

On the way down I saw many birds that I believed to buzzards circling overhead. I wrote a postcard to the folks at home saying among other things, "I saw two buzzards already." When I got home Marie greeted me with a statement, "Hah! You saw two buzzards already, eh! Do you think anyone cares? Do you know what we did with your card? We used it to clean up vomit from the car floor." Marie was Lucy and I was Charlie Brown.

Marie was not very fond of me and I guess I was not very fond of her. She had the impression that I always got more than she did because I was the oldest son and she was only a girl. She badgered me relentlessly throughout our pre-high school years. Like Charlie Brown, I countered with avoidance. This proved to be a good strategy with many people and situations I didn't like and I used it throughout my life. She became somewhat friendlier when in high school. She was one year ahead of me. She even fancied herself my teacher and protector. To some extent she was, and I was able to make many new contacts in school through her. She always had a bad temper, however, and the falling-out we had shortly after Dad died (over an old, broken-down cabin in Northern Michigan that she wanted the family to buy and restore) was permanent. Her last words to me were, "I'll see you at Mom's funeral." This was not to be. Marie died in 1974 at age 49 from a blood clot following surgery. Mom died in 1982 at age 77 from brain cancer. Marie generously left her estate to Mom, permitting Mom to live comfortably, but not lavishly, until her death.

I spent a week with the Gander family in Kentucky. They lived on a traditional Kentucky farm. The house had an ordinary A-shaped roof, but the porch roof coming off the bottom of the main roof was much shallower. This is a style that was seen all over the state. The house had no running water or indoor plumbing of any sort. Some of the bedrooms were on the second floor. The Gander family included a boy about my age. We slept upstairs. The first night, when all the family had gathered in the ancestral home to welcome Adolph and his new bride, the young boy and I were informed that it was time for bed. We went up and he showed me the chamber pot. It was a high, two-gallon, enameled container with a cover. He instructed me to kneel down and pee in the pot. The pot was standing on the hall floor. I did as he told me, but he neglected the part about aiming your pee on the side of the pail rather than on the bottom. As I peed into the empty container, a loud sound of pee hitting the bottom of the bucket and gradually changing in tone emanated as the bucket was filling. The conversation below halted. The silence was broken only by the sound of my pee. Finally a voice said, "Kebbie, what *are* you doing up there?" Then laughter.

I had a great time with the Ganders in Kentucky. They were very nice people. All told, four of the family, Adolph, his wife Bertha, Beth and Hattie worked at the Indian school at one time or another. Hattie was a very beautiful woman. She was my first grade teacher.

When we came home from Kentucky I brought with me a bunch of Kentucky Blue Grass and a hank of tobacco, raised by the Ganders. My playmates while I was at the Gander home included a Negro boy my age. I had never seen a Negro boy before. I thought he was very nice and enjoyed his company.

As a child, the only other Negro I knew was an architect, Louis A. Simon, sent to Neillsville in 1937 by the U.S. Postal Service to build a new Post Office building. Some city fathers were unhappy and asked to have a white man sent to do the job. Mr. Simon was denied a room at the local Merchant's Hotel. Dad was furious. He invited Mr. Simon to stay with us, which he did for a time. The Government, to its credit, said, "No Negro architect, no Post Office Building." The city fathers relented and Mr. Simon moved into the Merchant's Hotel. The Post Office building is used to this day, and in fact is on the National Register of Historic Places. The Merchant's Hotel is now an antique mall.

Mom and Dad were always very offended by social and racial injustices. During the Second World War, when West Coast Japanese-Americans were sent to detention camps, Dad learned of a Japanese family that would be willing to live and work at the Indian School. He invited them to be with us and they accepted. Mr. and Mrs. Mori and their daughter Mitsu worked at the school for several years.

We always said that there was a 'mark' on our house because tramps and hobos frequently stopped and asked for work or a meal. We always fed them and treated them with respect. Once a very sick and very filthy tramp, obviously suffering from diarrhea, stopped and asked for a meal. Dad said he looked like he needed more than a meal and asked him if he would like to stay until he got better. He agreed and Dad took him down to the Indian School, took him to a sick room, undressed him, bathed him and put him to bed. Dad then took the man's clothes down to the incinerator and burned them. A trip to the Missionary Barrel produced a new set of clothes and shoes. The man stayed at the school for several weeks until he was well again and then he departed with dignity and a new outfit.

Another annual visitor was a peddler with a huge knapsack that he carried on his back. He had no means of transportation except his feet. Everything he owned was in that pack, including the things he sold to make his living. Whenever he stopped to visit us, he was invited in to have a meal, to sell us a few things like sewing needles, and to tell us where he had been and about his adventures of the past year. To a little kid, it sounded like he was living a very exciting life.

****

Most of the time the Black River was a broad and gentle stream, so shallow that you could walk across it. If you jumped from rock to rock, and didn't slip off of any rock, it wasn't even necessary to get your feet wet. Sometimes, however, the Black River was high and wild. When the ice went out or it was in flood stage, it was dangerous to try to cross the river. The water roared and swirled, and when it went under the bridge, it boiled! When it was at its highest point in flood stage, it was about 35 feet higher than normal.

In 1937 when I was 11 years old, we had one of the worst floods ever in the State of Wisconsin. The river got so high that it flooded houses along the bank of the river, including the house where Gander and Bertha lived. Everyone was worried that the water, which was already up to the first floor of the house, would continue to rise until either the second floor would also be flooded or the house would simply float away. Some houses from upstream had already floated down the river, and when they collided with the bridge above Gander's house, had been crushed into a thousand pieces.

When it appeared that there would be a flood, Gander and his wife had moved all of their furniture to the second floor of the house. This would keep the furniture from being damaged if the water only flooded the first floor, but if the water got to the second floor or if the house washed away completely, everything would be lost.

In those days there was no television and no Weather Channel so no one had a good idea of what was likely to happen. We had to rely strictly on rumor. And the rumors came in. Some said that more rain was on the way. Others said the river had already crested. But no one knew for sure if the river had crested or if more rain was coming. What to do?

Finally a decision was made to tie a big rope to a tree on high ground, to take the other end of the rope through the floodwaters to the house and secure it to the porch railing. Using this rope as a "handrail", we planned to carry the furniture out of the house and place it on high ground until the flood receded. Everyone thought this was a good idea, so that's what we did. Everyone pitched in and helped, including me. I walked through the floodwaters to the house, hanging on to the rope for dear life. Because I was small and light, I had a hard time keeping on my feet and sometimes my feet were swept right out from under me. Then I just hung onto the rope until I could get my feet down to the ground again. It was real tough going.

When I got to the house, I picked up a piece of furniture, either alone or with someone else and carried it with one hand back along the rope to high ground. Coming back with furniture was easier than going to the house with nothing, because I was heavier when carrying the furniture and could stay on my feet better.

After a few trips we had moved all of the furniture out of that house and had it neatly stacked on high ground. We were very proud of ourselves. Now the river could continue to rise for all we cared. But that was not to be. No sooner did we have the furniture out when the flood began to recede. The rumor that the river had crested was correct. Moving the furniture had not been necessary, but we had no way of knowing that.

Had my father had known what I had done, I think he would have been very worried. I could have been swept away by the river and drowned. Dad didn't find out about this adventure until later. When he did find out about it he was not very happy. He said I should have let the grown-ups carry out the furniture. I thought I was grown-up when I was eleven. Dad said I had a ways to go before I was grown-up. He was right, but I didn't think so at the time.

****

1937 was a memorable year for yet another reason. Of course we were in the depths of the Depression, but we really didn't suffer because of the food, shelter and clothing provided by the Indian School. None-the-less, we longed for the days when the Depression would be over. Our mantra was that 'when Powell comes, we'll have black shoes and candy.' More on Powell later.

It was also in 1937 that a sculptor named Mr. E. F. Durig came to Greenwood, about 15 miles north of Neillsville, to create a monument dedicated to Gold Star Mothers and in memory of the 150th Anniversary of the Constitution of the United States of America. I have no idea who financed the statue. While the Durigs were in Greenwood, their daughter Rosemary, who played the harp, offered to put on a concert in Neillsville as a benefit for the Indian School. The date was set for a concert in the Neillsville Armory. Dad mustered us kids to peddle bills advertising the event and to sell tickets. Alas, the harp is not an instrument favored in the polka region of Wisconsin. The audience was very sparse in spite of our valiant efforts to promote the event. At the end of the concert, Dad presented Ms. Durig with a check that, I believe, was larger than the total take from ticket sales. The Indian School had also paid the rent for the armory. Some say that Rosemary found the love of her life in central Wisconsin while her Dad was sculpting.

****

I thought making hay was one of the best jobs on the farm in the summertime. We did almost everything on the farm with teams of horses. First the hay was cut with a horse-drawn mower. After it dried in the sun for a couple of days, it was raked into piles with a horse-drawn rake. There were two kinds of rakes, dump rakes and side delivery rakes. We had a dump rake. This was a rake that the driver rode on as he drove it through the hay field. When the rake was full of hay, the driver would step on a pedal and the rake would rise up and dump all the hay it had collected into a long pile. I enjoyed using the dump rake. It made me feel powerful to be handling horses and a big rake all by myself.

After the raking was finished, the hay was gathered by hand with pitchforks and piled high on a horse-drawn hay wagon. Tall men with long pitchforks threw the hay high up onto the wagon. A shorter person (like I was at that age) arranged the hay on the wagon, or drove the team of horses that was pulling the wagon. I liked driving the team the most. Arranging the hay required a lot of skill. The hay had to be arranged carefully so that it would not slide off the wagon as it jostled over the ruts in the field. Arranging the hay properly was a skill that took me a long time to acquire.

Since driving the team didn't require as much skill, I generally drove the team. The teamster, as horse drivers were called, sat or stood at the front of the wagon and directed the horses with long reins. If the teamster wanted the horses to start moving, he would say "Giddup" and shake the reins. If he wanted the horses to turn left he would pull the left rein. Pulling the right rein would turn the horses right and pulling back on both reins at once while shouting "Whoa" would stop the horses. As the hay was piled higher and higher on the wagon, the teamster would stand higher and higher on top of the hay.

One day after we had collected a large wagonload of hay and were heading back to the barn, we hit a large rut in the field. I was the teamster that day, and didn't see the rut. Anyway, we hit that rut hard and the wagon lurched first to one side and then the other and then it slowly tipped over and spilled all of the hay onto the ground. I was very embarrassed because I had truly made a bad mistake by not seeing the rut and by hitting it so hard. But the men who had worked putting the hay on the wagon just laughed and said they hoped I had learned something from this experience. I did! Always look where you are going and adjust your speed to the conditions. This lesson works even when you drive a car!

We put all the hay back on the wagon and headed for the barn again. This time we made it. When we got next to the barn under the big hay door, I stopped the wagon, got down and unhooked the horses from the wagon by pulling a bolt on the 'evener' and attached the 'evener' to the hay rope. Through a series of pulleys the hay rope was attached to a hayfork. The hayfork was stuck into the pile of hay on the wagon and "set" so it could hold onto the hay. Then I drove the team of horses down the lane and the rope in the pulleys lifted the hay up into the hayloft in the barn. When the hay was at the right place in the barn, a man inside the barn shouted for me to stop the horses. When the horses were stopped, the man in the barn pulled a "trip rope", the fork let go of the hay, and the hay fell into place in the barn loft. There it stayed until it was needed for the horses and cows during the winter.

I am telling all of these details because my younger readers will likely never see anything like this on a farm again. Today hay is put into bales or large rolls using big machines after it has been cut and dried in the sun. The bales are then loaded onto trucks with other machines and stacked by the barn under plastic covers. The rolls, which are also covered with plastic, are often left in the fields until some hay is needed for the livestock and then a roll is brought into the barn or feed lot using a tractor with a big prong on the front. Most farmers don't even own a hayfork, a hay rope or a team of horses anymore.

****

Loosening grain seeds from the stalks and heads of grain plants is called threshing. What remains of the grain plant after the grain seeds are removed is straw and chaff. Grains are used as food and straw is used for many other things like bedding for cattle and horses, but straw (and chaff) are not used as food since they contain very little nutritious material.

Grains are such good food that many animals and some people live on nothing but grains.

Today most grain is removed from the grain stalks with a large machine that travels through the grain field on its own power, and in one operation, cuts the grain stalks, knocks the grain loose from the stalks, separates the grain from the chaff and straw, puts the grain into sacks or into a large bin and returns the straw and chaff to the field. One man operates this combine, as it is called.

The first machine for cutting grain was called a reaper and was invented in 1885, by McCormick. His machine was a horse-drawn device that would cut down the grain stalks and bind them into bundles that could be picked up easily with a pitchfork and loaded onto a wagon. Mr. McCormick became very rich by manufacturing and selling his machine to farmers who could then more easily and more inexpensively harvest their grain. McCormick made a lot of money with his invention, but the farmers also made more money because they didn't have to hire as many people to harvest their crops.

But the invention of the reaper didn't solve the problem of threshing. It remained for someone else to invent the threshing machine. The threshing machine was a huge, complicated device into which the bundles of grain stalks were tossed. The threshing machine contained many mechanical flails that beat the grain off of the stalks, and a big grain-fanning mill that separated the grain from the straw and chaff. The threshing machine was powered by a huge tractor through a long belt that went from a pulley on the tractor to a pulley on the threshing machine. The tractor would also be used to pull the threshing machine from place to place when it needed to be moved. While it took many fewer workers to harvest grain with the horse-drawn reaper and the threshing machine, it still took more workers than most farmers had on their farms, even if the farmer's wife and all their children were counted. Some of the workers ran the reaper. Others drove the horses that pulled the wagonloads of grain bundles from the fields. Still others loaded the grain bundles onto the wagons, and several workers were required to operate the threshing machine, to throw the grain bundles from the wagons into the threshing machine, to move the grain bags into which the threshing machine discharged the cleaned grain, and to put new, empty grain bags under the discharge chute. Someone also had to tend the tractor. A reaping and threshing crew might include as many as 20 workers, but with the help of these machines, the 20 workers could harvest the grain from an entire family farm in a single day. Without machines, it would have taken perhaps twice as many workers more than twice as long to harvest the grain.

Where did the farmer get all of the people needed to harvest his grain, and where did he get the reaper and the threshing machine? Most farmers did not have enough money to buy these machines for use just once a year for only one day, and most farmers could not afford to hire the necessary 20 workers.

The solution lay in cooperation. Several farmers pooled their resources and together bought the necessary equipment, or one farmer went into the business of owning the equipment that he then rented to other farmers. During harvest season, the farmers would gather and together with their horse teams and their wagons, the reaper and threshing machine, would move from farm to farm as a group and harvest each farmer's crop. These groups of farmers and their teams and equipment were called threshing crews.

It was a very exciting day when the threshing crew came to the Indian School farm each year. When we were little children, all we could do was to watch and try to keep out of the way of the workers and the machinery. This was very important because the machinery was very dangerous. Many an experienced farmer was badly injured and some were even killed when they worked around the clanking machines. Sometimes, when we were older, we were allowed to drive the teams in the field and haul the grain bundles over to the threshing machine.

The farmers' wives also had a job to do. It was customary for each farm to serve dinner to the workers on harvest day. With so many people to feed, most farm wives would cooperate with each other just like the farmers did with the harvesting. Some of the wives would bake pies and cakes and others would bake bread. Some brought vegetables and others brought salads. The wife of the farmer whose fields were being harvested that day was expected to provide the meat dish. Often it was a dish made from animals butchered on the farm. Most farmers kept hogs, chickens, geese, sheep and cattle. Each of these could be used for the meat dish. Sometimes the farmer's wife would use meat from an animal that had been butchered many months ago; for example, she might use a ham from a pig butchered a long time ago. Hams were cured in salt and smoked for a long time. This kept them from spoiling and gave them a good flavor. Sometimes the farmer's wife would kill and butcher chickens on the morning of the harvest and give the workers a real fresh chicken dinner. Because 20 or 30 people couldn't eat a whole cow in one meal, cattle were seldom slaughtered simply to serve the threshing crew their noon meal. Remember, it was July or August when the harvest took place and very hot. Since few farmers had freezers, July and August were not good times to slaughter cattle. This was generally done in the winter when the meat could be kept cool out of doors until it was canned or otherwise preserved.

Sometimes, however, the farmer's wife would slaughter a young calf, and serve that to the workers. Veal calves are small enough so that 20 or 30 workers could easily finish one off during a harvest meal.

One year when I was old enough to join the threshing crew, we were having our harvest meal at the house of a farmer whose wife had butchered a calf for the meal. The meat was good, but it seemed kind of soft and fragile. One of the other farmers said to the host farmer, "How old was this calf when you butchered it? It seems kind of soft."

You know that veal should be tender, which is what makes it good, but it should not be too tender. Most calves are not butchered for veal until they are about two or three months old. At that time, they are just at the right stage of tenderness and they are also heavy enough to bring the farmer a good price in the market place. So what was host farmer's answer to the question? "Him got no old. Him come dead!" Apparently the calf was born dead so instead of wasting the meat, the wife butchered the dead calf and served it for harvest dinner.

All of this happened in the 1930s. By the late 1940s, threshing machines were a thing of the past. After WW II, combines replaced reapers and threshing machines. Some combines are pulled by huge tractors. Others are self-propelled. But the combines, just like the threshing machines of yore, are often owned by cooperating groups of farmers and each takes his turn with the crew and the combine.

The harvest noontime meal made by the farm wife is also a thing of the past. Mostly the harvesting crew sends out for a catered lunch served from a catering truck out in the fields, or the crew troops to the local fast food joint for burgers and fries. You can be sure that none of the burgers contain veal that's "got no old." Sometimes though, the hamburger might be tainted with salmonella. On the whole, however, while the harvest is not as colorful and fun as it was sixty years ago, it is a lot safer. Not nearly as many farm workers are mangled in the equipment as were when I was a lad.

****

Summertime was also time for Stucki Family Reunions. The first complete reunion was held in 1940 at the Indian School at Neillsville because in that venue there were enough beds, baths and dishes for everyone. The reunions lasted about a week. All of Grosspapa's children, their spouses and offspring attended. The descendants tree through the third generation included in this book conveys an idea of just how many people might be in attendance in any year. The 1940 reunion included 37 of a possible 43 attendees. By 1960, the fourth generation was very much in evidence. Naomi and I and our three children attended that reunion and had a great time. We missed the 1950 reunion because we were all tied up in graduate school.

My birth date and those of my 24 Stucki cousins range from 1917 to 1941 on a distribution curve that peaks in 1925. This meant that the cousins separated themselves into age cohorts rather than moving as a herd. Some cohorts liked to fish and play in the woods. Others liked more grownup pursuits.

There were activities for all, including visits to the Old Mission, where we would fish and swim in Dickie and Morrison Creeks and visit the Christian and the Indian cemeteries. My uncles and aunts would also visit with the Indians they had grown up with at the Old Mission. All of the Stucki uncles and aunts spoke the Winnebago Indian language, as well as German and English, so they could carry on conversation with the Indians in their native language. These reunions were the only occasions when most of the uncles and aunts could exercise their ability to speak Winnebago since most of them lived far away from Wisconsin, specifically in Ohio, Iowa, Indiana and Colorado.

One of the people visited was Miss Emma Manthe, who had been a teacher, maid and cook at the Old Mission at the turn of the century. She lived to be quite old and was always a joy to see.

Of course, we ate most of our meals together in the Indian School dining room and all helped with the meal making and cleanup, just like the Indian kids. Never to be forgotten was the song/prayer, *Danket Dem Herrn* (Thanks be to God), which was sung in four-part harmony, in German, before and often after the meal.

The reunions were also occasions when the cousins could renew acquaintanceships and try to impress each other. Sometimes we would visit each other's homes during the summer and the reunion was also an occasion to make such plans. I remember going to Waukon, Iowa to stay with cousins Don and Curt Stucki. One summer Don and I were fooling around in his kitchen pretending we were knife fighting, Errol Flynn style. We each had a table knife in our right hand and would grasp the opponent's right wrist with the left hand. Then we would try to 'stab' each other. Mostly we just moved around trying to gain balance advantage. All of a sudden there was a loud pop and Don's shoulder came out of joint. Apparently he had previously dislocated this joint playing football and it was prone to pop out. Uncle Frank had to take him to a doctor's office where he was given a whiff of ether to relax him so the joint could be popped in again.

The Grether and the Bopp kids were the oldest of my generation, so they often did things that we could only watch. I remember one time at the Old Mission when Jack Grether (born 1917) and Frank Grether (born 1920) were fooling around with a loaded BB gun. Each of them was trying to gain possession of the weapon. While they were struggling, the gun went off. Frank had his thumb over the end of the muzzle. He yelped and fussed when this happened. I was just watching and wondering how it would all end. This probably happened about 1934 when they would have been in their teens. I would have been eight and differences between our ages seemed to be very large.

Today Frank and I are close friends and our ages seem to be about the same.

One or two days of reunion would be spent at Lake Arbutus, a dammed up part of the Black River between Neillsville and Black River Falls. The lake was always the color of root beer because of the tannins it contained. The water was very clean however, and fine for swimming. In 1940 we went to an area where no one else could be seen. We called the area Stucki Beach. Many years later we tried to lease the land comprising Stucki Beach but found that the power company that owned the shore was no longer leasing land to private people because someone had filed suit when the dam remained closed and their cottages were flooded during high water. Some years later the power company began to lease land again, but we were no longer interested. Stucki Beach is now occupied by several fine cottages, and is for all intents and purposes, a private beach. During the 1960 reunion, we swam at the public beach on Lake Arbutus in Hatfield.

During the winter of 1947 some of us cut logs at the Old Mission that we were going to use to construct our cottage on 'Stucki Beach'. The logs were ultimately used for the construction of the house Mom and Dad lived in on the north side of Highway 10.

In the 1930s, the road to both 'Stucki Beach' and the Hatfield beach was a small, one-or two-lane, sand road that crossed several small streams emptying into the lake. Single-lane steel bridges spanned the creeks. One day as we were crossing one of these bridges on our way to the beach, we saw someone floating upside down in the water near the shore. Dad stopped the car and together with some others, who were also attempting to cross the stream, pulled the body of a stout old Indian woman out of the water. As they turned her over to see her face, Dad said, "Why that's Mary Yellow Thunder!" And it was. The story unfolded as the sheriff was called and the whereabouts of Mary on the evening before was determined.

Mary Yellow Thunder was a war widow entitled to a government check every month. She was a lonely old woman and liked to drink in the company of others. Her government check arrived and was cashed the day before her death. As always, a couple of her male friends showed up to help her spend her money. As always, they went out and bought some booze. After drinking it up they decided to drive down to the beach. They came to the bridge and instead of crossing it, ran into the railing. The impact threw Mary against the dashboard and cracked her head. Her 'friends,' thinking she was dead, threw her into the stream and took off. As I recall, the coroner thought she may still have been alive and that she drowned. I don't know what happened to her friends. We called the bridge Mary Yellow Thunder Bridge until it was replaced some years later.

During reunions, fish for breakfast was a ritual always observed. The fishermen would go out early in the morning and catch enough fish for all. The fish included bass, walleyes, Northern pike, some crappies and bluegills and maybe some trout. Uncle Heinie and Uncle Jack were just a bit contemptuous of those who fished for anything other than the wily trout, but they ate all species just as the rest of us did. There is nothing quite like bread and butter, fried fresh fish, blueberries and coffee for breakfast.

We also picked wild blueberries during the reunions. Blueberries were quite abundant in those days and it was not difficult to collect many gallons in an afternoon. How to get the berries back to Colorado, Iowa, Indiana and Ohio was a problem never satisfactorily solved. I remember one plan that turned disastrous. Someone got the bright idea of mixing the berries with oats, hoping that the oats would absorb the juice or something and the berries could be floated away in water later. It turned out that both the blueberries and the oats sunk and had to be laboriously separated.

****

Bumpie might be a strange name for a dog, but our Bumpie was a large, lumbering "bump" of a St. Bernard that the family acquired when she was just a little puppy. But little she would not remain. While she was growing up she really didn't know her own strength and once had chewed on little brother David until he was screaming with pain. It was only because Dad happened upon the scene that Bumpie didn't do in David completely.

As Bumpie grew into adulthood, she became jealously protective of David and his little sister, Betty. Bumpie would accompany them wherever they went, prevent them from crossing the highway or going into the river, and protect them against any approach by strangers or aggressive acquaintances.

This later proclivity was to be Bumpie's undoing. After David started school at the Indian School, his friends would taunt the dog by feigning an attack on him. Her tormentors would approach first from one side and then the other. The poor dog would become frantic, and finally became mean and belligerent to everyone except members of our immediate family.

One day a laundry soap salesman came to the school and stopped to talk to David and Betty on his way to see Dad to try to sell him some soap. Bumpie decided that the salesman was going to harm David or Betty so she bit the salesman, not hard, but enough to keep him away from the kids and enough for the salesman to mention it to Dad. The salesman told Dad he had an offer Dad couldn't refuse. If Dad bought seven cases of soap, the salesman would forget about the dog bite. The soap was terrible. It wouldn't get clothes clean and

73

turned white sheets a dull yellow. Mom decided it was time to get rid of Bumpie.

A dog pound was out of the question. For one thing, there was no such thing as a dog pound in Neillsville. If there had been, we wouldn't have wanted to see Bumpie "put to sleep." After all, she had been with the family for years. Mom searched for a sympathetic farmer who needed a watchdog.

The first candidate was a bearded patriarch who had homesteaded a farm far out in the "boondocks," the backcountry far from town. The patriarch had a large farm with all of the accouterments of a turn-of-the-century homestead. He had a granary, a smoke house, a hen house, a slaughter house, a hog barn, a cow barn, a horse barn, two silos, a barn with a hay loft, three teams of horses, goats, cows, geese, ducks, chickens and guinea fowl. In the smoke house hung hams, slabs of bacon and smoked sausages.

We sorrowfully bade goodbye to Bumpie after delivering her to the man's farm. A day later she was home again, wagging her tail and slobbering joyfully, telling us how glad she was to see us. She had traveled about 14 miles on unfamiliar roads to make the journey from the farm to our home. We mournfully loaded Bumpie into the station wagon and drove back to farm.

The farmer was not pleased. Bumpie had been put into the granary when she was delivered the day before. Before departing for her old home, Bumpie had destroyed several sacks of oats, spread the grain all over the immediate area and chewed the door off the granary. The farmer needed a watchdog, however, and reluctantly took Bumpie again.

The next day Bumpie was back with us. The farmer phoned us and told us Bumpie had broken out of another shed and then broken into the smoke house for a meal of smoked ham before making the journey home for the second time. Not content to eat just the one ham required to satisfy her hunger, she chewed on several other hams, sides of bacon and rings of sausage. The farmer was beside himself with rage. "I never want to see that beast again. Don't be surprised if I file suit," he shouted. To his credit and our everlasting relief, we never heard from him again. No suits were filed.

Bumpie's next assignment was turkey farming. She was judged to be a perfect turkey guard by Mom and by a farmer who raised ten thousand Thanksgiving turkeys a year. She was given a large doghouse, to which she was chained, and was placed in the turkey field some distance from the farmer's house. Her job was to bark when anybody or any marauding animal threatened the turkeys. The farmer would show up with his shotgun when Bumpie barked. Twice a day he visited her to provide food and water.

The last time I saw Bumpie she was standing by her doghouse with a sad look on her face. I left for the Navy and Bumpie was dead of old age before I returned for my first leave. I think Bumpie actually died of a broken heart. She did not want to be removed from her family, but Mom had little choice. With the conditioning she had gotten from the children who teased David and Betty, she had become too dangerous to keep at our home on the school grounds.

****

One of my summer chores as a teen was to drive the truck to the Old Mission, pick up a load of firewood and drive it back to the Indian School. I would unload the wood into a shed next to our house for use in the kitchen stove and a small heating stove in the basement. The wood was mostly jack pine cut from the Old Mission property by Uncle Jack, who lived there in one room of the Mission home for several years. The wood was very soft and light. It burned rapidly without producing much heat, but it was easy to split, and

Uncle Jack split many cords each season, much of which I hauled to Neillsville.

Uncle Jack lived a very lonely life, possibly by choice. He also lived a very frugal life. When I visited him while hauling wood and was invited to have a meal with him, for example, bacon and eggs, he would fry the bacon and eggs in a frying pan, transfer my serving to a clean plate and transfer his to a plate he used regularly without washing. At the end of his meal he would simply mop out the remaining food with a piece of bread and return the plate to its special storage place. The frying pan and coffee cup were given similar treatment. He said washing dishes for himself was a waste of time, soap and effort.

****

Powell! I have no idea where that name came from, but it apparently referred to an invention or maybe the inventor of a system for capturing power in reciprocating engines. The phrase, 'when Powell comes, we'll have black shoes and candy' really referred to a company called Lever Motors Corporation, and 'when Powell comes' meant when we all got rich from our investments in Lever Motors Corporation. I have no idea why we fixated on "black shoes and candy."

The Lever Motors Corporation was incorporated in 1929 and was dissolved in 1935 for non-payment of taxes due. A second company was incorporated in 1935, also called the Lever Motors Corporation. This company was in existence until 1955, when it was also shut down as result of an injunction obtained by the SEC. The SEC charged that stock had been offered to the public without proper SEC permission. Officers and directors and their families had contributed about 1/3 of the total money invested in the company. No fraud had been committed. The charge was simply failure to register. By 1955 the company was flat broke and in debt, and the principals were aging rapidly.

Lever Motors Corporation died, not with a bang but a whimper.

No story about the Indian School would be complete without at least alluding to Dad's role in the fortunes of the Lever Motors Corporation. I have no idea when he became seriously involved with the company, but some years before its demise, he had been elected president. For a short period of time in the early 50s, I was acting secretary of the corporation.

During the years of Dad's involvement, he enthusiastically spoke of the Lever invention to his friends and relatives. As a result, many of them invested in the company, including some of his children. I think I invested a total of $2,600, some of which I had borrowed from Dad. I paid him back in full shortly after I left the University of Wisconsin and got a job in the real world. It would be interesting to know how many other Stucki relatives became investors. I have lots of paper from Lever Motors Corporation, but I don't have a list of stockholders. I think that was kept very secret.

The people involved in Lever Motors included R. P. Rainey and his brother C. F. Rainey of Black River Falls, Cliff Shaffer the engineer/plant manager, and P. J. Moe of Glendive Montana. I knew all of these people and found them sincere and dedicated, but in the case of the Raineys, perhaps a bit naïve and slightly paranoid. When one of the Raineys was reminded that gas turbines might just replace the Lever concept as a means of extracting power from fuel, he responded with, "Well, we'll just put a Lever in the turbine!" The Raineys were also convinced that General Motors and other big boys were destroying us because they feared our wonderful invention. As a result, the officers refused to give control of the company to any outside investors, something that seemed to be required for commercialization. They were convinced that the large investors would close the company to keep it from being successful. They may have been correct.

Cliff Shaffer was a brilliant engineer and succeeded in developing many ideas in Diesel design that yielded patents. When the company went belly-up, Cliff got all the patents, engine parts and office furniture in lieu of back pay. I remember that one of his inventions was for a pre-combustion chamber. I wonder if any of these patents ever saw commercialization.

Several Lever gasoline and Lever Diesel prototype engines were constructed and tested in the laboratory and under field conditions. I remember once seeing a car in our driveway with a Lever gasoline motor installed. I think one of the Rainey brothers was driving it, but it may have been Cliff Shaffer.

My guess is that Lever Motors was destined to fail because the invention was just too complex. While the Lever concept had some thermodynamic advantages, the number of moving parts seemed to be excessive. On the other hand, for complexity, look at today's internal combustion engines. I wouldn't dream of fooling around with anything under the hoods of modern cars. Their complexity is daunting.

****

Although deficit of knowledge and memory makes the effort less than perfect, I must acknowledge the roles that many others of the Stucki Clan besides Dad and Mom and many of our friends played in history of the Indian School. Dad's youngest brothers, Henry and Jack, were heavily involved in construction at the school in addition to working as regular employees in other capacities. Uncle Jack was also gardener for many years. He also built the "Stone Steps" leading from the school to our house. Henry (Uncle Heinie or Uncle Billy to us) was the school's and the family's engineer/carpenter.

He built the playhouse in addition to lots of other things. We kids used to pester him constantly with questions while he was working until he would say, "'Supposin' you all run along and play now." That was the signal to leave. When we wouldn't leave while he was building the playhouse, he threatened to knock it down with a 2x4, so we left. Auntie Irma, Henry's wife, was employed at the school and I think that is where she met him.

Of course, Jack Grether and his wife Marie, were prominent contributors to the school in the later years as was Auntie Mia Grether, Jack's mother. Cousin Frank Grether often helped with the various projects at both Neillsville and the Old Mission. Margery Moser, a relative of Uncle Cal's wife, I believe, also worked at the school. And to be sure, every one of my brothers and sisters and even sister Peg's husband, Bud Bremer, worked at the school at one time or another.

Besides the relatives and other employees I have already mentioned, there were dozens more. Most were recruited from Evangelical & Reformed churches around the country. They accepted employment as an act of faith rather than as a means of making a living. Their pay was astonishingly low and their dedication impressive.

Several Indian men and women, mostly graduates of the school, were also employed at one time or another. One of my favorites was Johnny Winneshiek. He was a patient, intelligent and hard-working man. I regarded him as my buddy though he was many years my senior.

Fred Vornholt, Mark's son, also worked at the school. When we were freshmen in High School, Fred, Roy Garvin and I were county grain-judging champions. We must have learned something about agriculture at the Indian School.

Chapter V – After World War II

Most of what I have written thus far took place before 1940. In that year I graduated from eighth grade and the next fall I enrolled in Neillsville High School. Roy Garvin was the only Indian to attend high school with me in Neillsville. After our freshman year he transferred to a different city. Although my life revolved around high school and activities in town, I continued to reside at home and knew pretty much what was going on at the Indian School. Then came the Second World War. Much changed in the years 1941-1946.

Many of the Indians with whom I had gone to school entered the military and fought for their country. Many did not return having made the ultimate sacrifice. I will always be very impressed with the dedication and sacrifice that the Indians demonstrated in World War II and the Korean War. Their contributions are all the more noteworthy considering the raw deal given them by the country they served with such distinction. Mitchell Red Cloud, Jr., one of my classmates, was awarded the Medal of Honor for his valor. The Indian Cemetery near the Old Mission is named in his honor.

When I was a senior in high school I turned seventeen and took an exam for entry into the Navy V-12 program for pilots and deck officers. I passed the exam and entered the Navy on March 1, 1944. My first assignment was to Purdue University where I took the first year (8 months) of engineering. Then I went on to Illinois Institute of Technology in Chicago for my second 8-month year of engineering. I was then sent to Glenview Naval Air Base north of Chicago, where I did a variety of jobs like tearing down old engines and starting Yellow Peril airplanes on the flight line. That fall I was sent to Pre-Flight School at Iowa City, Iowa, then to Ottumwa, Iowa, and finally to Flight School at Corpus Christi, Texas. By then it was April of 1946 and the war had been successfully concluded. The

Navy decided it didn't need any more pilots. Any of us who insisted on learning how to fly would have to sign up for 4 more years. The alternative was to go home immediately. I chose the alternative and returned home in May of 1946. I remember being on the train as it approached Neillsville and crossed the Black River above the Indian School. It was early morning. As I looked out from the train window at the School and at my home, I remember thinking: did I make a mistake by returning home?

But, I thought, it really didn't make any difference. Howie Warnock, a Navy buddy, and I were planning on going to South America to seek our fortunes. This would be an exciting life. We had become acquainted with several Brazilian Naval Cadets who were training with the U.S. Navy and were assured that they would be most helpful to us if and when we arrived in Rio. But this was not to be.

Shortly after I returned home, Dad had a heart attack that flattened him for several months. In 1946 there were not many drugs or procedures available to treat coronary artery disease besides bed rest. As I was standing by Dad's bed one day, he asked me to stay home for a few months to get the school in shape for the coming year. Much maintenance had been deferred due to the unavailability of materials and workmen during the war years. What could I say but yes? I immediately called up Howie and asked him to help me at the school and he readily agreed.

We worked all summer and when fall came, it seemed natural to both of us that we return to college to finish our degrees. Howie had one more year for his engineering degree and I would be a junior. In September he returned to Cleveland and I enrolled at the University of Wisconsin. The next two summers were spent working at the Indian School and the winters at the University. After Howie finished his degree he took an engineering job and no longer worked with me.

In addition to Howie, my brothers and sisters helped with most of the projects. The summer of 1948 was really my last contact with the Indian School. In the fall of 1948 I enrolled in Graduate School at Wisconsin and married Naomi. Howie was our best man. We remained friends with him and his wife, Ruth, until his death from a stroke in March of 2003.

I mention all of this as a part of the Indian School narrative, because description of what we did those three summers can provide some additional insight into life at the Indian School.

During those summers, we painted the entire inside of the school and varnished all of the woodwork. The walls were sand float finished plaster and had never been painted. The dry surface absorbed primer at a ferocious rate. We bought Porter Perfect oil-based paint in five-gallon buckets and put the paint on with brushes. Rollers were not common at that time, and there was no such thing as latex paint. The finish coats were done with regular semi-gloss oil-based paint that we tinted ourselves. We fashioned a perforated phonograph turntable platter into a paint mixer by bolting it to the end of a rod. An electric drill made paint mixing a snap.

We also tried to paint the outside wood on the school building but did not have the equipment to reach the top of the fourth floor so Dad agreed to hire professionals. They did a nice job.

We did manage to seal the roof, however. We climbed out of the fourth floor windows to get to the roof instead of using very long ladders. The roof was covered with asphalt shingles, many of which had tears and missing parts, but Dad was convinced that we could save the roof simply by covering it with liquid asphalt. So this is what we did. The material we used came in five-gallon buckets, of course, and contained suspended aluminum to made the roof shine and reflect the heat. Over a period of a couple weeks we got the whole roof painted and the loose singles pasted down. The roof didn't leak, but it looked terrible. It was impossible to put the asphalt on evenly so the roof had the appearance of a badly made patchwork quilt. Our asphalt paint job served for many years before the roof had to be re-shingled.

While we were fixing the roof we saw that the main boiler chimney and the chimney for the kitchen were both in bad shape. Each had to be taken down to the roof and rebuilt. Brothers Ben, Bill and I did this job without any expert help. It was quite a task. We even poured new caps for these out-sized chimneys.

Included in the summer projects at the Indian School was the sanding and refinishing of all the wooden floors in the building. This was a very tough job because there were many floors made of fir. These floors did not sand and refinish easily, but they had to be done none-the-less. The problem was the slivers. Fir is prone to produce slivers.

****

During the summer of 1947 we remodeled the house at the Old Mission and built a parsonage for the new minister Mitchell Whiterabbit. Until that time, John Stacy was the Evangelist for the Mission and lived in the Old Mission home, the one in which Dad and my uncles and aunts had grown up. When John Stacy retired in 1946 and moved to his farm in Greenwood, Wisconsin, it was clear that a new parsonage would be required for the new minister, Mitchell WhiteRabbit. Uncle Billy, who had earlier become a professional carpenter/contractor, was engaged to build the house, and I was to be his assistant.

Charles Round Low Cloud, who wrote the "Indian Report" column for the Black River Falls Banner Journal, followed our work with great interest. He reported that many of the Ben Stucki family worked in various capacities on that project as well as on the co-op store. From the August 20,

1947, issue of the Journal – *"Rev. Ben Stucki and family were here from Neillsville Indian School and Mrs. Marie Grether, one of Rev. Stucki's sisters. Last Monday Mrs. Stucki and Mrs. Marie Grether were working in the house, Mrs. Grether painting too, and Jacob Stucki, Benne Stucki and Frank Grether are working cement block, at the store, and new house did not finished yet, they said they have to send for metals needed."*

A collection of Mr. Low Cloud's columns has been published: *Charles Round Low Cloud, Voice of the Winnebago,* by W. L. Clark & W. D. Wyman, University of Wisconsin-River Falls Press, 1973.

While we were building the parsonage and co-op store, and remodeling the old house, we lived in a part of the old house. Miss Louise Kippenhan (sister of teacher Cilla Kippenhan), who functioned as the Mission social worker lived in another part of the large house. Since we were removing old chimneys, some of the rooms were open to the outside. Bats like to hide during the day and would go into the house through the chimney openings. In the evening they would generally leave the house to hunt for insects, but sometimes they would stay.

One night when I was trying to sleep, one of the bats that decided to stay indoors for the night was bothering me by flying around my bed and making flapping noises with his wings. I decided to catch and kill the bat. This was a bad idea from a conservationist standpoint, but I didn't know it at the time. So I chased the bat, caught it and killed it and then took it outside. I had to get up anyway to go to the bathroom. We didn't have an indoor bathroom, so we had to go out to the privy in the back of the house.

I took the dead bat and went out to the privy. After I had deposited the bat by the side of the privy and finished peeing, I returned to the house, only to discover that the door to the house had locked itself. Now that wouldn't have been so bad except for one thing -- I slept "in the raw" as they say, and didn't have any clothes on. Not having clothes on in the dark was OK, but it was early morning and starting to get light. What to do? Well, I went out to the tool shed, got a screwdriver and removed the door so I could get back into the house before Miss Kippenhan awoke.

During the summer when we built the house, Frank Grether had come out of the Navy and was studying botany at the University of Wisconsin. That summer he spent collecting plants in the sand country around Black River Falls. He also lived at the Old Mission and would sometimes help with the building. I also remember him helping to paint the Indian School roof.

Brothers Ben and Bill often worked with me. One notable time was when we had to build a septic tank in the backyard of the new parsonage. I suggested that brother Bennie should dig the hole for the tank. It was to be constructed of blocks on a slab on concrete to be poured in the bottom of the hole. Bennie asked how much time would be required to dig the hole. I replied that I thought it would take a man a day to dig the hole, so, as a teen, he would probably require two days. Actually we both worked almost a week before we managed to get the concrete slab poured and the first blocks laid. The problem was that the area was pure sand and it was a dry summer. No matter how far out we dug, sand would always pour into the bottom of the hole before we could get a form set or concrete poured. We finally had to put in retaining walls to keep out the sand. "It should take a man a day" was a constantly heard quotation on the job.

Bennie and I also built the chimney for the house. The pitch of the roof was rather high because the house was designed to have a small second floor under the main roof. This meant the chimney had to be quite high to reach beyond the roof peak and properly draw smoke from the fire below. After starting the chimney in the basement we finally emerged from the roof. After putting up a scaffold upon which to stand and work, we built the requisite 6-foot tall chimney above the roof. After the scaffold was taken down it was apparent that there was a twist in the chimney that had gone undetected earlier. The problem was that I had only a short level and could not detect the emerging error while I was laying brick. The twist remains to this day and probably no one but me knows or cares.

Another project was the re-wiring of the church building after it was struck by lightning, probably in 1947. The lightning stroke fried most of the wire in the bell tower and on down. While I was up on the roof working, Charles Round Low Cloud, appeared below and interviewed me for his column, but I have been unable to find his report on that subject.

That summer we also put some amenities into the old house where Grosspapa had raised his family. The amenities were for Miss Kippenhan. In one room we installed an integrated kitchen unit consisting of a sink, a stove and a refrigerator. We set it in a room without adequate light so it was necessary to cut out a place for a window. When we set about this task, we found that the wall was about 18 inches thick and that it consisted of very large logs. With hand tools, we managed to get an adequate hole cut and a window installed, but it was a horrendous job.

In 1952, the old house burned to the ground. An Indian woman who was living with Miss Kippenhan apparently left an iron unattended and the fire was started. In addition to destroying this historic building, the fire destroyed many of the documents associated with the Mission's early years.

The Mission Church, originally located several blocks from the new parsonage, was moved to the site of the now-destroyed house, next to the parsonage. It was attached to a new parish house type of building that was used for meetings and lodging for a Mission worker. The church/parish house, the parsonage that Uncle Heinie and I built, and the Christian Cemetery are all that remain of the Old Mission.

In 1965 after the Wisconsin Winnebago Tribe received Federal recognition, the Board of Missions of the Evangelical and Reformed Church made 103 acres of its 120 acres at the Mission available to the tribe for construction of low-income housing. The Winnebago Indian Mission Church continues to own the remaining 17 acres. Many nice homes now surround the Mission grounds

Chapter VI – The End of it All

About the time I finished working at the school during the summers between my illustrious Navy career and college graduation, officials in the Evangelical and Reformed Church (later to become the United Church of Christ) began to engage in serious discussion about the appropriate fate of the Indian School at Neillsville. It had become clear that a boarding school for Indian children was no longer needed since Indian access to public schools was becoming more certain.

Church officials decided that the Indian School would become the Winnebago Children's Home, a licensed welfare agency, and would function as a refuge for disadvantaged youth of all races. The Home would be owned and supported by the church, but regulated by the state. For the most part, the courts would decide which children would be sent to the Home and the state would pay for their care on a per child basis. Accordingly, a new charter was established in 1954 together with a new Board of Directors and a new administration. Dad became what might be considered CEO of the operation and my cousin Jack Grether became Chief Operating Officer. When Dad was about to turn 65, he decided to retire. He approached his board and the church about his prospects.

It was at that time that he discovered that he had only been given retirement credit by the church for the years that he served **after** he had been ordained into the ministry. His ordination had occurred about halfway through his tenure at the Indian School, after he had studied independently for his theological examinations at the request of the church fathers. Because he was not credited for all of his years of service, the amount of money he would receive from the church in retirement would hardly suffice. The church offered to keep him on in a job that involved traveling to churches all over the country to raise money for the new endeavor and to allow him and Mom to live in the house west of Highway 10. He and Mom had little choice. He stayed on and died on the job in 1961 at the age of 68.

As soon as the new charter was established, government regulations regarding structure and management of the school were applied at great expense. Structural changes in the main building were made to comply with new building and safety codes. It is my understanding that children could no longer participate in any work at the home because that would be regarded as exploitation. All clothing and other supplies were to be new, not used. The ratio of workers to children of about 1 worker for every 5 students became about 4 workers for every one student. I never saw a child outside when I visited my mother during the 1960s and 1970s. Apparently nobody ever sledded down those beautiful hills anymore, and certainly none of the kids at the home ever went fishing by themselves in the Black River. I understand that staff carefully supervised all recreation. Perhaps this could not be avoided, given the nature of the children sent by the courts to the school.

When the new status of the Indian School – first called the Winnebago Children's Home and later, Sunburst Homes – was established, a new house for Mom and Dad had been built on the north side of Highway 10, across from the main building. Dad wanted a study in the otherwise rather small house and the Board agreed, provided he and Mom financed the construction of the study. This they did. After Dad died, the Board gave Mom 10 acres on top of the east hill near the east boundary of the school property. This was in payment for the contribution Mom and Dad had made for construction of the study. On this property Uncle Billy built a small home with a picture window that allowed Mom to look out over the beautiful vista that is the Black River Valley. She lived in this house until she died in 1982.

****

What of Sunburst Homes, nee Winnebago Children's Home? After I married and entered graduate school and ultimately moved from Wisconsin, I knew very little about the progress of the institution. Jack Grether retired after a few years and other administrators came and went. The place became very secretive in the name of privacy for its clients and we (the Stucki children) were allowed only cursory glances at the structure and operation of the Home. Mom lived close by and felt very offended by what seemed to be going on there. She felt, perhaps with some justification, that the administrators that came after Jack were incompetent at best or dishonest at worst. I have no idea where the truth lies. What I do know comes from newspapers and other accounts.

Early on, the Home undertook massive fund-raising efforts to finance the building of a number of what they called "group homes" where the children could live as if in a family unit rather than in an institutional setting. Each of the group homes had several 'mothers and fathers' to manage the children. In addition there were social workers and teachers and psychologists and guards. In 1968 the Home dedicated a very nice recreation hall and classroom building. One the front wall was a large, beautiful, cast brass plaque identifying the building as *Stucki Memorial Hall*. Some years later that plaque was removed. No one I have talked to seems to know what happened to it. I have heard that the building was renamed *Kippenhan Hall*.

In about 1999-2000, a huge administrative center called the Orville Hoffman Center was built just north of the main building on the old ball field. The price tag was alleged to be one million dollars. Sometime in the 1990s the whole enterprise began to come apart. The Orville Hoffman center was never occupied. An account of the dissolution of Sunburst Homes is recorded in the Clark County Press. It details how the Lutheran Social Services organization of

Wittenburg, Wisconsin, took over the management and operation of Sunburst Homes and how this group tried unsuccessfully to sell some of the group homes and the farm across the river. Finally Lutheran Social Services abandoned the site of Sunburst Homes and moved the remaining children and some of the staff to a new location on the east side of Neillsville.

The owners of Sunburst Homes, the United Church of Christ (or one of its subsidiaries), declared an inability to pay its many debts and defaulted on its mortgage. The entire property was sold at Sheriff's auction to the State Bank of Withee, Wisconsin in April 2002 for $1.06 million. This partially satisfied a $1.3 million mortgage held by that bank. I am told that the United Church of Christ assured the bank and other creditors that they would be paid in full what they are owed, eventually.

In March of 2003, the main school building was razed after a short delay caused by some clerical error in the asbestos removal permit. Gone are the dormitories, the class rooms, the kitchen, the boiler room, the tool room, the dining hall, the peeling room and all the other memorable places described in this account. The barns, the slaughterhouse, the milk house and the other original outbuildings had been demolished years before.

From my perspective, the one bright feature of the demise and demolition of the Winnebago Indian Mission School was that by the time of its demise, the entity had shed all association with the Stucki Family. The last time I visited, the guard and others I met said that they had never heard of anyone named Stucki. So it goes.

The Winnebago Indian Mission School at Neillsville

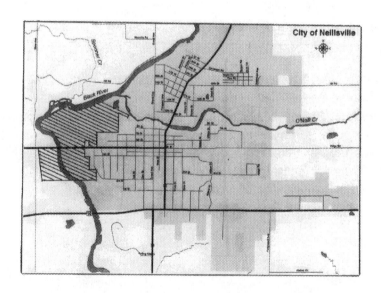

Map of the City of Neillsville – 2002
Hatched area approximates School property
within and outside of city in 2002.
Map reprinted and modified with permission of the
Clark County Wisconsin Government

Old Mission church and parish house in the 1950s after
Grosspapa's house burned

Old Mission parsonage in the 1950s
Built by Uncle Billy in 1947

Kippy's classes in "Sunday best"
circa 1937

Classmates – back of school visible at left, barn at right
circa 1935

More classmates – note bearing race on banister
circa 1935

And still more classmates
circa 1935

Learning to milk cows – circa 1939

Performing the Babcock Test for butterfat – circa 1939

Grain judging champions
1940

Sawing firewood - circa 1935

The farmhouse where we were born and raised

Mom's and Dad's last house built around 1950

Mom & Dad as Indians

River rocks for jumping

Stucki Family Is United for First Time Since 1914

From far and near, 37 members of the Stucki family wended their ways to Neillsville last week for the first family reunion since 1914. The Winnebago Indian school formed the base of operations, with side trips made to the Old Indian Mission, near Black River Falls, to Lake Arbutus and Wedges creek.

Evenings were passed in seeing motion pictures of relations and reviewing the work of the Rev. Ben Stucki family with the Winnebago Indians here. Memories of years gone by were brought back as the reunited members sang many of the songs as they had sung them in their childhood days, at home in the old Indian Mission in which their father, the Rev. Jacob Stucki, ministered to the spiritual and physical needs of the Winnebago Indians for 46 years.

All eight of the children of the Rev. Jacob Stucki were present. Six are married, and their children total 24. Those present from the immediate families were:

Dr. and Mrs. J. C. Stucki and three children of Denver, Col.; the Rev. and Mrs. Ben Stucki and seven children of Neillsville; the Rev. and Mrs. Frank Stucki and two children of Waukon, Ia.; Mrs. Carl Bopp and three children of Youngstown, O.; Mr. and Mrs. David Grether and two children of Decatur, Ind.; Johanna Stucki, R. N., of Youngstown, O.; and Mr. and Mrs. Henry Stucki and child of Neillsville.

Others present were: Mrs. Otto Dietrich, the only living aunt, Mr. and Mrs. Elmer Dietrich and Mrs. Lily Rhode, all of Plymouth; and Vernon and Janet Hoesly of Council Bluffs, Ia.

All members of the family were present except Mr. Bopp and two children of Youngstown, O., and three Grether children of Decatur, Ind.

Newspaper clipping reporting the 1940 reunion

Reunion 1940

All the cousins

The whole gang

An approximation of the mealtime song
sung at reunions

The melon eaters

Ben's and Frank's broods
July 1935

With Grandfather Kehrli
July 1934

Cal's and Ben's kids
July 1933

Ben's and Dave Grether's kids
At Lake Arbutus
Stucki Beach
August 1933

The stone steps from our house to the school
built by Uncle Jack

The Ben Stucki family at home
in the early 1940s

The spring ice breakup
under the Highway 10 bridge

The spring ice breakup
under the railroad bridge

Betty, David, Billy and Benny with Bumpie – circa 1941

On the roof of the play house
built by Uncle Billy
July 1934

The Lever invention

AT THE 1960 REUNION

The Grether clan

Stuckis and their spouses

The Ben Stucki clan

More Grethers

The Bopp clan

Mary Ann Grether & Naomi Stucki with their kids

"Just Fooling Around"

"Bathing Beauties"

At Lake Arbutus during the 1960 reunion

Henry & Cal

Peeling Logs for the 'Cottage'
1947-1948

Neillsville Post Office – 2003

Merchant's Hotel – 2003

Mom and Dad
on the Old Stone Face

Demolition of the Old Indian School
March 2003
Photo reprinted with permission from the
Clark County Press

Two Generations of Grosspapa's Descendants

Jacob Stucki 1857-1930
+Anna Marie Reineck 1862-1894
      William Zwingli Stucki 1887-1912
      Lydia (1) Marie Stucki 1889-1892
      John Calvin Stucki 1891-1980
      +Marie Sophia Lahr 1898-1992
            Bonnie Marie Stucki 1927-
            +Charles Re 1926-
            Magdelyn Lahr Stucki 1929-
            + Francisco Sabichi 1927-
            John Calvin Stucki 1937-
            +Arlene Johnson 1937-
      Benjamin Stucki 1893-1961
      +Ella Amanda Kuester 1905-1982
            Marie Ann Stucki 1925-1974
            Jacob Calvin Stucki 1926-
            +Naomi Edith Bersch 1922-
            Esther (Peg) Johanna Stucki 1928-1999
            +Clarence Bremer 1919-
            Benjamin John Stucki 1930-
            +Joan Kay Russell 1931-
            William Paul Stucki 1931-
            +Barbara Martha Rude 1931-
            David Richard Stucki 1935-
            +Dawn Eloise Neilson 1937-
            Elizabeth Barbara Stucki 1936-
            +Clarence Ernest Brown 1934-
+ 2nd Wife Johanna Reineck 1865-1903
      Frank Stucki 1895-1961
      +Hulda Margaret Kehrli 1893-1975
            Donald Frank Stucki 1925-1983
            +Diane Hutchinson 1934-
            Curtis William Stucki 1928-
            +Elizabeth Ross Cowart 1946-
      Lydia (2) Johanna Stucki 1896-1989

+Carl Frank Bopp 1893-1956
>>Calvin Charles Bopp 1918-
>>+Gretchen Tiefert 1920-
>>Carl Norman Bopp 1919-
>>+Marion Evalina Pratt 1920-
>>Frank George Bopp 1921-
>>+ Maxine Hanan 1924-1988
>>Lois Marie Bopp 1922-
>>+Theodore Roosevelt Draper 1921-2000
>>Helen Louise Bopp 1925-1971
>>Janice Carolyn Bopp 1929-1990
>>+Donald L. Jones 1927-1991
>>+ 2nd Husband Charles Gettman 1930-
Anna Marie Stucki 1898-1975
+David Grether 1889-1945
>>Jacob William Grether 1917-1998
>>+Marie Hildebrand 1915-
>>Hermina Marie Grether 1919-
>>+ Calvin John E. Stuebbe 1917-
>>David Frank Grether 1920-
>>+Daisy Elizabeth Sanford 1926-
>>+ 2nd Wife Mary Anne Trace 1923-
>>Ruth Johanna Grether 1922-
>>+Albert Vincent Gress 1920-
>>Grace Margaret Grether 1923-
>>+Chester Ploeger
Jacob Stucki Jr. 1900-1956
Johanna Stucki 1901-1988
+Edward Spire 1892-
Henry William Stucki 1903-1966
+Erma Olm 1909-
>>Irma Marie Stucki 1938-
>>+Ronald Markus 1937-
>>John Jacob Stucki 1941-
>>+Judith Eggert 1942-

Note: Spouses shown are either only spouse or spouses with children from this marriage.

Dedication

and

Acknowledgements

This book is dedicated to the Winnebago Indians, a tribe badly mistreated by the white people of their country. In spite of this mistreatment, the Winnebago people are fiercely patriotic and defend their country with vigor and courage in times of conflict. It is with great respect for their culture that I dedicate this book. Early in my life with the Indians, I had only scant appreciation for their dignity, wisdom and patriotism. With maturity, my admiration for them has grown.

My daughter Marcia Stucki provided valuable help with the manuscript at all stages of its development. She acted as critic and editor and provided much encouragement to undertake the project. Thanks also to my cousin Curtis Stucki who provided the initial impetus. His continuing help with genealogy has also been appreciated.

Thanks also to Eugene Gutknecht, Director of the Jackson County Wisconsin Historical Society; Mary I. Murray-Woods, Historian at the Jackson County Public Library; Mick Kuzjak, Editor of The Clark County Press; Jay Shambeau of The Clark County Government and my deceased Mother, Ella Kuester Stucki, who was an inveterate 'saver' of family pictures and documents.

A special thanks also to my wife Naomi Bersch Stucki, who endured long periods of silence while I sat at my computer or pondered my writing problems.